# moral education
# in
# theory and practice

# moral
# education
## in
## theory and practice

## by robert t. hall
## and john u. davis

ℙℬ *Prometheus Books*
Buffalo, NY 14215

Published 1975 by Prometheus Books
923 Kensington Avenue, Buffalo, New York 14215

Library of Congress Card Number 75-21078
ISBN 0-87975-052-9

Printed in the United States of America

For Marianne and Bobbie, Martha, Karen, Beth, Kristin and Lauren.

# Contents

Preface    9

1  The Moral Domain    13

2  Education Without Indoctrination    27

3  An Integrated Approach    45

4  Philosophical Analysis I: Principles and Priorities    57

5  Philosophical Analysis II: Universals and Ideals    71

6  Psychological Analysis I: The Psychology of Moral Development    85

7    Psychological Analysis II: The Humanistic Classroom    111

8    From Theory to Practice I: The Case Study Method    127

9    From Theory to Practice II: Moral Concept Analysis, Games,
and Simulations    151

10    Conclusion: Five Theses on Moral Education    171

Bibliography    179

# Preface

We have written this book for two reasons: first, to provide a general introduction to this new field of education for interested students, teachers, administrators, and others; and, second, to attempt to restore something of a philosophical perspective to the field as it is now developing. In carrying out these objectives we have necessarily directed ourselves toward two distinct audiences—students and teachers to whom the moral domain is a new field of interest and our colleagues already at work in this area. At first we felt that this diversity of objectives and audiences might be incompatible, but it seems in retrospect that it has been good to have both groups of readers in mind. We feel that it is important at this point for theorists and educators in the field to discuss their differences within the context of a programmatic statement of what they take to be the nature and scope of moral education. At the same time consciousness of writing for our colleagues has helped to keep us honest with those for whom we hope this volume will be an adequate first introduction. The marriage of general and specialized objectives has thus, we feel, been a happy one, although like all good marriages it has had its ups and downs.

Were it not for the support of institutions this work would not have been possible. We are grateful to the National Endowment for the Humanities for a fellowship (for Robert T. Hall) and to Bethany College for a sabbatical (for John U. Davis) which allowed us to pursue this study together in Oxford, England, during the academic year 1972-73. We are indebted to several theorists at work in this field but especially to Mr. John Wilson, Professor R. M. Hare, Professor Paul Kurtz, and Professor Barry Beyer. We should like also to express our thanks to the educators who participated in the Moral Education Workshop at The College of Steubenville, especially to Professor John Susky for his advice and encouragement. We owe special thanks to Dr. Claudette Diomedi for her help with the text —help which in many cases clarified our thinking as well as our writing. She has spared the reader a lot of confusion and some nonsense, although she is not responsible for what remains of both. Finally we must thank Mrs. Josie Kuzma for her help with the typing, and two students, Cindy and Sandy, for keeping the circus running.

Bethany, West Virginia
July 1975

# moral education
# in
# theory and practice

# The Moral Domain

This is a book about moral education—a new concern for a very old issue. We are interested basically in the decisions people make about their own actions and in the ideals and values upon which those decisions are based. We intend to propose an approach to education in this area of life—moral decision-making—because we believe that people, especially young people, should be given some help toward doing a better job of it.

Making decisions about what to do is an everyday human activity. Some decisions of course are more important than others, but many of our seemingly small daily decisions are really quite important because they affect other people and because they constitute, little by little, the kinds of lives we are building for ourselves. And deciding what to do is often a complicated activity; it involves many different aspects of our personalities— thinking about facts, sympathizing with the feelings of others, predicting the consequences, loving, and often hating or simply being afraid. Decision-making is nevertheless a distinct and important aspect of life, an aspect we shall call the moral domain.

The term "moral" requires some clarification, however, because it has been increasingly misused over the past half century. In everyday discussion it has come to be identified almost exclusively with matters of sexual behavior. We read in the newspaper, for example, that someone has been arrested on a "morals" charge, and we have little doubt as to the general nature of the accusation. In other decades the term was used in a similarly narrow way with reference to alcohol and gambling, and in light of current affairs one could guess that it might come to be used exclusively to refer to political corruption. But this limitation of the meaning of the term "moral" to specific topics or areas of human behavior only reflects the poverty of our thinking. It shows the extent to which our decision-making has become compartmentalized so that our decisions about these topics are separated from the consideration of basic principles and values. In fact, the result of compartmentalization is that we never really reflect on our decisions from a perspective which allows or helps us to develop values and principles. Instead we concentrate on specific issues such as sex or politics, and as a result many of us never develop what really might be called a moral perspective.

Moral education as we see it, therefore, should not be confused with sex education. Problems of sexual behavior are indeed important but so are decisions that must be made about military service, occupation, civil rights, and lifestyles. In this book we are concerned with the whole range of personal and social decisions. The basic assumption of our approach is that no single problem area of human behavior can be treated in isolation and that the whole scope of human behavior needs to be related to the consideration of moral values and principles. If sex education needs a moral dimension—and we certainly believe that it does—this can only be provided through education in the whole of the moral domain. Our interest at this point, therefore, is centered at the most basic level of moral thought, the first steps, so to speak. We believe that education at this level can be most effective if the more volatile social issues such as sexual behavior, abortion, and civil disobedience are postponed as subjects for classroom discussion at least until students have had some practice at attacking less explosive moral problems. Only when the ability to consider issues rationally and calmly is developed in a class can students profit from considering the more difficult issues over which even thoughtful adults are divided. We shall not, therefore, have anything to say about the moral dimension of sex education, except that it ought to be considered in the light of all that we have to say about moral education itself.

In its original and rightful sense the term "moral" refers to issues for which consideration of values or principles are relevant. A moral question requires the kind of thinking which seeks to establish a relationship between one's particular decisions and one's values or principles. Concentrating on this domain in its own right, as we propose to do educationally, thus militates against the fragmentation or compartmentalization of our thought and action. It can help us to see how our decisions and actions in one area of life are related, through the general values or principles we hold, to decisions on other matters. It can help us, therefore, to bring our daily decisions under the guidance of a more comprehensive view of life and thus to build a more coherent lifestyle. At any rate, it is in this more comprehensive and traditional sense that we shall use the term "moral" in referring to the "moral domain." Should the reader have difficulty with this term or with the phrase "moral education," let it at least be clear that we are talking about education in personal and social decision-making and in the principles, ideals, and values upon which intelligent human decisions are based.

The term "moral" is also frequently used in an evaluative sense to mean morally right as opposed to morally wrong or immoral. When some particular action is spoken of as being the "moral thing to do" in a certain situation, what is implied is not merely that it is a question of right and wrong, but that it is the *right* action. The sense in which we shall use the term, however, is the equally common descriptive sense in which "moral" signifies that a certain question or problem is one which *involves* issues of right and wrong. The term is used this way whenever a particular dilemma is described as a "moral problem" or when we say that someone faces a "moral decision." Moral education, therefore, is not education simply in the right things to do (taking the term in its evaluative sense), but rather education in the nature of moral thinking and in the skills and abilities of decision-making.

## MORALITY AND SOCIETY: THE CURRENT STATE OF THE MORAL DOMAIN

There has certainly been a great deal of concern in recent years about people's behavior. Social commentators have been warning us for some time that we live in an age of moral crisis. This is probably true, at least to some extent, but we need not debate the point here. What is more important is to come to a clear understanding of exactly what is meant by the phrase "moral crisis" so that we can form some idea of the relationship between the moral domain as a realm of individual decision-making and what we see happening in the social world around us. At any rate a brief analysis of the notion of a moral crisis may help to clarify further what we mean by the moral domain.

It may well be true, as we are told almost daily, that there is more deviant behavior in terms of crime, sexual abnormality, divorce, tax evasion, and political corruption than in the past. While such behavior may bring about a social crisis, disrupt the social order, precipitate a political crisis, or threaten the rule of law in a state, it does not alone constitute a moral crisis. Morality concerns the ideals and values that underlie people's actions, and deviant behavior does not necessarily mean that a person has changed his moral beliefs. Changes in social behavior in fact may be based upon strong rather than weak moral convictions. The social disruptions of the civil rights movement in the 1960s were largely the product of strongly held moral principles. And even now people are advocating and undertaking radical changes in their personal and social lives—changes which deviate from the social norm and which may indeed develop into crisis proportions—for what they consider to be moral reasons. Therefore, a moral crisis cannot be said to exist on the evidence of deviant behavior alone.

Nor is a moral crisis, strictly speaking, a matter of people failing to live up to their moral principles and values. This is indeed a most serious problem, but it is a question of a general or widespread failure of will, of losing the heart to persist in one's convictions, or of a loss of morale (not morals). When such loss of will is widespread, it can foster an attitude of "Well I don't really approve, but everybody else is doing it," which makes it difficult for individuals to hold and act upon any moral principles at all. Yet this problem is more of a psychological crisis than a moral one—a question of what Aristotle called backsliding or of what might now commonly be called courage, integrity, or conviction. And as with the notion of deviant behavior it assumes that people do hold some moral values—some principles to be lax about or some standards to slide back from—not that their moral beliefs are themselves in question. The problem is thus psychological, or even spiritual, rather than moral.

In contrast to the person who knows what he believes to be right but just cannot bring himself to do it, a person who has a genuine moral problem is in doubt about what he thinks is right. A moral crisis, therefore, is a state of society in which many people have, for one reason or another, lost their sense of what is right and what is wrong. It is not that they have adopted new moral values which are offensive to their neighbors or that they cannot quite live up to the moral values they do hold. It is rather that for one reason or another they no longer believe in the traditional values or that they cannot apply them to the problem they face. Whether moral beliefs are understood to be based upon religious convictions or simply upon personal ideals, it is confusion about the beliefs themselves that constitutes a moral crisis.

This distinction can help to clarify what we mean by the moral domain: when people who hold different moral beliefs disagree about what behavior ought to be allowed or disallowed in their society, the crisis is a social or political one; when people who hold definite moral principles and values fail to put these ideals into practice, the crisis is a psychological or a spiritual one; but when people don't know what values or principles they hold or are uncertain of how to apply their moral ideals to specific situations, the crisis is a moral one. All three are serious, but the center of our concern in the pages that follow is the moral domain. We are interested in helping people understand their own moral values and principles and in helping them determine the application of those values and principles to a lifestyle.

It can also be helpful, in trying to assess the state of the moral domain in our age, to consider some of the causes of the difficulties we are experiencing. A moral crisis—and we are still concerned with the *nature* of the current malaise rather than with its extent—is not generally the kind of thing that occurs by design. The people who live in ages of moral uncertainty are not usually responsible for getting themselves into a dilemma. More often than not, moral uncertainty is due to changes in the conditions of life, so that the principles which have guided men's actions in the past somehow do not seem to fit the present situation. Rather than rejecting traditional values and principles, they simply do not know how to apply them to the new problems.

In the realm of medicine, to cite only one example, technical advances now make it possible to preserve the biological functions of life far beyond the point at which a few years ago a person would have died. Doctors are uncertain even from a legal perspective when a person ought to be judged dead, and most of us are uncertain about whether such extensive machinery ought always to be used or not—especially to extend biological functions when the effort to save life really is hopeless. The point is that we have not asked for this difficulty, nor have we gotten ourselves into it by default. It has arisen as advances in medicine have occurred. We are in doubt about what to do, but not necessarily because we have given up the traditional moral principles. We still believe that we should do all we can to preserve life and relieve pain, but now we are uncertain about the application of this principle when preserving life (and we are no longer sure exactly what is and what is not life) seems futile, and we cannot preserve life and reduce pain at the same time. The problem, however, is not one that we have consciously brought upon ourselves, nor is anyone to blame for being morally lax or for not holding or wishing to hold moral principles. The difficulty arises because modern medical technology has changed the situation: with the expansion of what *can* be done, it has become less and less clear what *ought* to be done.

Nor is this situation unique. Behind a great many of the personal difficulties one would characterize as moral problems today, we can find scientific or technological changes which raise doubts about the meaning and application of traditional moral principles. The changes themselves, as with the progress in medical techniques, are undoubtedly good, but they are creating many moral difficulties. And not all of the changes we have seen in recent years are a result of scientific progress. Some are merely social changes such as the increased educational and occupational independence of women, a side effect of which is that divorce is a more reasonable alternative than it ever was for our grandparents. As a result the traditional moral beliefs about marriage and divorce seem not to have the force of reason they once had. Many people find themselves confused; they believe in the permanence of marriage from which it follows that divorce is somehow wrong, but at the same time they may well know of situations in which divorce seems the right thing to do.

But while the moral crisis of our age may produce a great deal of confusion and perplexity, we should not be too quick to look upon the situation as hopeless. Although serious men and women in our society may be less clear about what values they hold and about the application of those values to new and problematic situations, they are not necessarily indifferent or morally obtuse. In many ways people seem to be making a sincere effort to rediscover or reconstruct values and ideals which will be adequate guides to life in this age. Indeed, some commentators have seen the civil rights movement, the war protests, and the women's liberation movement of recent years as indications of a new and heightened moral awareness on the part of large sections of our society. There may thus be as much reason for encouragement as there is for shock and concern.

It is in this context and as a response to this crisis that the possibility of moral education has been discussed in recent years. A clear understanding of the nature of the crisis is most important, however, for an adequate appreciation of the proposals that have been made and of the alternative we intend to suggest. We have emphasized that the crisis is a product of the changed conditions of life and that, much as one might wish it, the principles and guidelines that seemed immutable for our grandparents and parents cannot always be made to answer questions or provide directions in the world as we know it. If this is the case, however, moral education *cannot* be viewed merely as an effort to inculcate traditional principles and values. We cannot approach the business of moral education as though the crisis is merely backsliding that can be remedied by a reinforcement of traditional values. What needs to be done in terms of moral education is to teach young people, and ourselves, to think through moral problems more carefully, to consider the meaning and the significance of the traditional moral principles in the light of recent changes, and to reestablish principles, values, and guidelines for ourselves.

Perspectives on this problem differ considerably. Some people are convinced that the best process for reestablishing a foundation for ourselves in the moral domain is to reconsider and reevaluate the basic values that have been handed down through our religious and cultural traditions. Others believe that the best way is to begin with experience and let new principles evolve from individual decisions. The difference between these approaches, however, may not be as great as it seems, for in the process of reevaluating and rediscovering traditional values we must test them in experience. Either way, in a time of moral uncertainty we need to reconsider the reasons for our actions, not merely to judge whether those actions conform to traditional norms or rules. The objective of moral education, as we see it, cannot be simply the inculcation of accepted values and standards. We must aim, rather, at developing in students the *ability to think* about their own values, to relate decisions of right and wrong to ideals of a coherent and principled lifestyle.

This, at any rate, is what we shall call the moral domain—the realm of decisions about human actions, along with the principles, values, and ideals by which intelligent decisions may be guided. By so defining the moral domain we have already begun to develop an aim or objective for education in that we attempt to develop in young people the ability to think about their own decisions and actions in a rational way; in other words, to consider the values and principles on which their decisions, actions, and ultimately their lives are based.

Isolation of the moral domain for educational attention is not, as we mentioned at the outset, a new idea. The history of conscious efforts at moral education goes back to Plato and Aristotle. In some cases, as with Plato, these efforts were openly indoctrinative. Aristotle's perspective, on the other hand, was remarkably close to the view presented here. Not only did he consider it "a matter of real importance whether our early education confirms us in one set of habits or another," but he also believed, as we do, that the best kind of moral education is experience and practice in making moral decisions.[1] As a man becomes a master builder by experience, he argued, so people become just or unjust, brave or cowardly, through their dealings with others in situations that present them with these decisions.

From a historical point of view it is remarkable that our society has paid so little direct attention to moral education—certainly less than any society in history. It was assumed, of course, that the churches would undertake the role of moral educator and that the field had best be avoided in the public schools because of the radical separation of church and state. Today both of these assumptions are false. The churches certainly cannot fill the role of moral educator for all citizens since an increasing percentage of Americans either are not church members or do not take the moral teachings of their religions seriously. But the second assumption—that public education must avoid the moral domain—is equally false, since, as we hope to show, the moral domain can be effectively isolated and treated educationally in its own right without endangering the separation of church and state.

From time to time, however, people in our society have urged the idea of moral education in public schools upon us. In 1909 John Dewey wrote a book in which he argued that the schools have a much-neglected moral responsibility to society. "The school," he said, "is fundamentally an institution erected by society to exercise a certain specific function in maintaining the life and advancing the welfare of society. The educational system which does not recognize that this fact entails upon it an ethical responsibility is derelict and a defaulter. It is not doing what it was called into existence to do."[2]

Citing precedent and the advice of philosophers about moral education, however, is not enough. Before jumping into the task of constructing a program for moral education, we should answer for ourselves a number of serious questions concerning the nature of this domain and its place in our system of public education. We can only proceed with our proposal if we are ourselves satisfied, and can convince our reader at least to entertain the possibility, that moral education can indeed be undertaken in a way that is consistent with the principles of education as they have evolved in our society.

## MORAL EDUCATION AND RELIGIOUS EDUCATION

In approaching the issue of public moral education it might be best first to clarify our view of one other question; the relationship of morality to religion. Obviously, the moral domain we have described is related to what is generally recognized as religion; for many people religious belief is the source of their value commitments or moral principles. Some readers will doubt, therefore, that one could possibly deal adequately with moral principles and values without considering the religious basis of such beliefs. While we sympathize to a great extent with this perspective, we do not think that the tie between morality and religion is necessarily so firm that a separation of the two domains for educational purposes is impossible. One might recognize the essential relationship between moral values people hold and their religious beliefs and still make a serious effort to focus attention on the moral values themselves. The manner in which moral commitments are based upon religious beliefs is itself a religious question and must be dealt with in that context. *We shall, therefore, begin with the assumption that there are such things as moral values and principles which guide the decisions we make*, and we shall try to treat *all* moral beliefs as well as their religious foundations, if they have such, with respect.

Our intent in this proposal should be clear: we are convinced that for educational purposes morality and religion can be separated and hope that others likewise may be convinced as they consider the nature of the moral domain more fully. If it seems to some readers that we have left out the all-important religious aspect of morality, we can only say that although we recognize and acknowledge the fact that religious beliefs provide an important source of moral principles for many people, this area of human thought is not our particular concern at present. We do not deny the need for education in the religious domain, nor do we propose moral education as an *alternative* to religious education. We shall assume, however, that the domain of moral values and decisions can for educational purposes be separated from the religious beliefs which may surround and support it. Only when this separation is firmly established are we willing to propose that the moral domain can and should be included in a public education curriculum.

There are, in fact, some rather clear precedents in other disciplines for the separation we are proposing. Religious beliefs often affect people's interpretations of history, but this has not prevented educators from teaching history while avoiding the arguments for and against viewing history as the unfolding of a divine purpose. Similarly, in science it has been found quite possible to teach a considerable body of knowledge concerning the nature of the world without raising questions of the ultimate reality, origin, or purpose of the universe. In the past, objections have been raised in both these areas to the separation of the religious dimension from the secular, but in both it has proved to be a viable division of human thought—at least for educational purposes. We believe that the same is true of the moral domain and that moral education can be undertaken in ways which avoid conflict with religion and do not denigrate religious beliefs. We should acknowledge, therefore, that people hold certain moral principles and beliefs for many reasons, both religious and nonreligious, and that both religious and nonreligious world views which underlie moral values are important and should be treated with respect. Our particular focus, however, will be on the nature of the values and principles people hold and the way these values and meanings function as guides to human decisions rather than on the sources or foundations of these values.

## EDUCATION IN THE MORAL DOMAIN

Having identified and described briefly what we take to be the moral domain, we must now finally say something about why we consider education in this domain an appropriate concern for public schools. On this score two questions deserve to be answered. First, what is the relationship of this domain to the current objectives of public education? And, second, how can moral education be undertaken in a manner consistent with the principles of a free society? Actually, we cannot answer either of these questions satisfactorily until we have explained exactly what we are proposing, that is, until the reader becomes more fully aware of our approach. But it still may be helpful to say something at the outset about how we think these questions ultimately will be answered.

Education in citizenship, as we now have it in most public and private schools, falls far short of adequately equipping young people to be effective participants in a democratic society. Although a reasonably successful effort may be made in communicating some idea of the basic structure of our government and the history of our country, little attention is given to the personal and social values upon which our democratic institutions are based. Education in this area amounts to a very superficial treatment. Youngsters learn only that people hold, or are supposed to hold, values such as honesty, equality, and freedom without ever learning what these values themselves are or how they are important to the development of a democratic lifestyle or society.

It is important to note, however, that it is not by any official plan that education in these basic personal and social values is lacking; textbooks on American history and civics are often very explicit about the communication of values as one of their objectives. As one teacher's manual for a civics course puts it, "Perhaps the most urgent problem we face today is our need for a deeper understanding of, and commitment to, traditional American values."[3] The public statements of educators and national leaders reflect the same idea. According to Merrill F. Hartshorne, executive secretary of the National Council for the Social Studies, "A prime function of our schools is to develop enlightened citizens who believe in the values of a free society, who know our history and understand our system of government and who are alert to the significance of developments on the international scene."[4]

The real issue of moral education in public schools, therefore, is not *whether* basic values and decision-making are intended to be taught or should be taught. The real question is rather *how* they are to be taught and whether education in this domain is really effective or not. As soon as we get beyond the flowery phrases of our educators and public leaders, it becomes apparent that the objective of education in the basic values of our society is more a matter of rhetoric than of practice. We find repeated mention of values and principles in textbooks and teacher's manuals in civics and history, but we have yet to find a book that actually tells students what a value or a principle is. Ideals such as justice, liberty, and equality are mentioned as though students already know what these values are; never are they discussed directly or exemplified. It is apparently presumed that students acquire value concepts indirectly from the subject matter. We doubt, however, that this happens as regularly or as thoroughly as might be desired. In actual fact the teaching of the values and ideals of our tradition is for the most part left to chance.

Leaving the communication of values to chance, however, poses difficulties for the average social studies teacher. If the teacher does recognize and accept responsibility for education in values and decision-making, he soon discovers that he must be more explicit about values than the textbook and that he can only do this effectively by relating the content of the course to current issues. But it is precisely at this point that he feels, and rightly so, that he may be depending too much on his own opinions or his personal understanding of the values involved. Having gone beyond his resource material in order to accomplish the real objective of that material, he finds himself without educational guidelines and perhaps without a clear understanding of the nature and application of the values and ideals he wishes to communicate.

The situation is even worse with a teacher who does *not* experience some personal anxiety on this issue. He is either ignoring this part of his task entirely by teaching only the "hard facts" of the subject or assuming that his own values are exactly the same as those upon which any democratic society is based and consequently teaches his own opinions as though they were the only truth. This approach, or absence of one, is the most common form of indoctrination.

The need for better education in the moral domain is thus apparent when one considers the overall objectives of public education and the current practice of avoiding this area. It is certainly part of the intent of public education to teach the values and ideals which underlie the institutions of our society. Our performance, however, falls far short of our objective, and it is this shortcoming that the present proposal for education in the moral domain is intended to help correct.

If the aim of moral education is accepted, this still leaves us with the question of whether the task can be accomplished in a manner that is consistent with our traditional commitment to individual freedom or not. One important principle of public education in a free society is, of course, that individuals ought to be free to adopt their own moral (and religious) beliefs. We certainly agree with this principle and intend, as we hope will be evident from the nature of our approach, to construct a program for moral education which will safeguard the freedom of the individual. The difficulty is not so much with the principle, however, as with the way it has been implemented, that is, with the official policy of laissez-faire, which assumes that people are most free when their education in the moral domain is left to chance. This policy has kept educators from dealing effectively with the moral domain and has created the impression that anything more than merely mentioning values and beliefs is forbidden in public education. The official laissez-faire approach has certainly not produced the desired results, for rather than leaving young people free to opt for one particular moral stance or another, it has encouraged them simply to avoid considering their own moral principles or to give mere lip service to common value concepts such as justice, liberty, and equality without really understanding their implications. Rather than creating a situation of greater individual freedom in the area of moral beliefs and ideals, the official laissez-faire policy has produced what amounts to a shallowness of thought and commitment. As a consequence we are developing a society of men who pledge their allegiance to rather high ideals but who seem hardly to understand, and certainly not to accept, the consequences of their own principles. Past ages of religious and nationalistic indoctrination may have produced bad results in terms of individual freedom, but the age of official laissez-faire has not done much better. If young people are not presented in one way or another with some substantial moral values or ideals, they do not necessarily go on to develop their own principles. They come, rather, to neglect moral commitments entirely and then fall under the influence of the behavioral fashions and styles of the day, until popular trend, the "thing to do," takes the place of values and principles entirely.

In this context we pose the basic question of education in the moral domain: If it is true that people in our society suffer from a lack of moral guidance—a shallowness of thought that results in part from the official public school laissez-faire policy—can we do something educationally to restore moral thought and commitment without eliminating personal freedom? If leaving the task of moral education entirely to chance does not fulfill our objective, then we must find other ways of educating in the moral domain, ways which bring young people to a realization of the nature and importance of moral principles to human life without compromising their freedom. While one cannot claim that the present proposal will accomplish this with complete success, we define it as our objective.

This formulation of our objective indicates the direction of our approach. We have specifically raised the question of the possibility of education without indoctrination in the moral domain because we take this to be the most important *educational* issue. Others have approached moral education from the perspective of psychology or from the field of moral philosophy. While these perspectives are important in providing the essential tools of the task, we think that an effective and acceptable plan for moral education must be guided by the requirements of educational practice in a free society—specifically, by a principle of education without indoctrination. Our proposal begins, therefore, in the following chapter with a discussion of the principles of education without indoctrination. In later chapters we will outline a specific program for education in the moral domain based upon this understanding of the nature of education and drawn from the most significant philosophical and psychological contributions to the field.

## NOTES

1. Aristotle, [Nichomachean] *Ethics* (Baltimore, Md.: Penguin, 1953).

2. John Dewey, *Moral Principles in Education* (Boston: Houghton Mifflin, 1909), p. 7.

3. *Teachers Manual and Answer Book: Citizenship and Government in Modern America* (New York: Holt, Rinehart and Winston, 1966), p. 1.

4. Merrill F. Hartshorne, "The Teaching of Civics Today—For the Citizens of Tomorrow," in Bard, Harry; Moreland, Willis D.; and Cline, Thelma N. *Citizenship and Government in Modern America* (New York: Holt, Rinehart and Winston, 1966), p. v.

2

# Education Without Indoctrination

Moral education, like education in other value-laden subjects, such as sex and politics, poses many different kinds of problems, some practical, some social, and some theoretical. Effectively communicating a particular concept to students by certain teaching techniques is a matter of educational method. The ability of students at a certain age to understand a concept at all is a psychological issue. And desirability of teaching certain subjects such as moral decision-making in public schools is a social issue, that is, one to be determined (in democratic states at least) by some manner of public consensus. The issue we shall face in this chapter, however, is a theoretical one. We have already attempted to make a case for the importance and the desirability of moral education; we must now attempt to show the theoretical foundation upon which such education is possible.

The problem can perhaps best be formulated as a question: Can moral decision-making be effectively taught without simply indoctrinating students into certain prescribed or accepted beliefs and behavior? Is it not all, inevitably, a matter of brainwashing? In order to answer these questions adequately we shall have to state the educational criteria which govern our proposal both in its conceptual formulation and in its practical implementation. More, then, is at stake here than an effort merely to put aside possible criticism: we are attempting to formulate our own educational guidelines and, of course, to make them explicit.

## INDOCTRINATION

It is almost inevitable that one serious objection to any proposal for moral education would be stated as an objection to "indoctrination." Although the term "indoctrination" has not always been used to express disapproval of the teaching in question, this is its dominant meaning today, and we shall use the term in this sense. As Professor Ernest Horn wrote in 1937, "To brand any act of teaching as propaganda or indoctrination is to damn it in the eyes of the educational world."[1]

To say that indoctrination is wrong, however, implies a definite value judgment about indoctrination; therefore, it might be best to make the nature of our judgment explicit at the outset. We take it that indoctrination is wrong, both educationally and morally, because it hinders or thwarts an intellectual process which any individual has a right to exercise freely or autonomously. If the indoctrination of factual information is in question, then men have a right by virtue of their intelligence to confront not only some one chosen theory but also the whole available range of information and opinion and to make up their own minds. If the indoctrination of moral beliefs and judgments is in question, then, we say, people have a right to make their own moral decisions without having their intellectual efforts thwarted, pressured, or coerced. This right to make one's own moral decision without coercion or pressure is a correlate of the concept of individual responsibility upon which our legal and social systems are based. If we hold people morally responsible for their own actions, as we do legally, then people have a right to decide for themselves whether they will act in certain ways or not. Or socially, if we hold people responsible for their own behavior, as we do when we praise or condemn their actions, then people have a right to as great a degree of freedom as they can attain in deciding about these actions. Since indoctrination diminishes the freedom of human thought and action, it is wrong—at least in any society based upon these freedoms.

Although the term "indoctrination" connotes disapproval, it should not be abused as a term of criticism for any system of education which one dislikes. Some people, for example, speak with great approval of "education in the traditional ideals and values of the American way of life" and with equal disapproval of the "indoctrination of young people in Communist nations." But the Americanism of the one system no more assures the fact that education is conducive to freedom of thought than the Communism of the other demonstrates that it is a system of indoctrination. If American ideals and values are inculcated so that they are believed in a narrow-minded fashion by students who refuse even to consider the possible merits of other ways of life, this is indoctrination and not education. In the end if it is simply the handing down of values and ideals from one generation to another that occurs, then either Communists educate as do Americans, or Americans indoctrinate as do Communists. The same criterion must be applied to each.

One other qualification on the use of "indoctrination" is necessary. While it is now commonly supposed that indoctrination is by definition morally wrong, some philosophers and educators have hesitated to accept this usage because most people clearly do approve of some educational practices which seem to be cases of straightforward indoctrination—practices such as the direct inculcation of social behavior in rearing small children. We see little difficulty with this position, however, because according to the common pejorative meaning of "indoctrination," the training given to small children cannot be called indoctrination at all. Children are and must be taught a great deal of behavior by their parents and teachers well before they reach a stage of development where they are ready for what we speak of as moral education, that is, for learning to make their own moral decisions. This early childhood training is both necessary and inevitable. People do not grow up in a moral vacuum; they grow into a family and a community where certain norms of behavior (mores, as they are sometimes called) prevail. Parents pass on to their children their own ways of living along with their feelings and beliefs about their actions. Teachers inculcate—and rightly so—the kind of behavior necessary for the social organization of the classroom. And when young people begin to make conscious decisions for themselves and to undertake responsibilities, it is always within (or against) this background of early training. The importance of this early learned behavior differs from person to person, but its effect should not be underestimated. At any rate it is understood, as William H. Kilpatrick pointed out long ago, that "the child's education cannot wait until he is mature enough to decide for himself."[2]

To speak of all this childhood training as "indoctrination," therefore, is unnecessarily confusing. If indoctrination is commonly understood to be morally wrong, it is because it hinders or thwarts decision-making which ought to be autonomous by virtue of the human being's responsibility for his own decisions. And if this is what is commonly implied, as we think it is, we should really only talk about the possibility of indoctrination when youngsters are psychologically mature enough to make their own decisions. As Professor R. M. Hare has said, "indoctrination only begins when we are trying to stop the growth in our children of the capacity to think for themselves."[3] Since one can hardly stop or hinder an activity of which children are not yet capable, we need not speak of this early childhood training as indoctrination. There are, of course, many ways in which early training can be detrimental to the future development of mature or autonomous thought, but we could find other words to express our disapproval without calling this indoctrination. It seems to us best, therefore, to reserve this term for the inhibition of mature decision-making and to find other language for training prior to what has been called the age of responsibility.

In suggesting this we do not assume that any single point or stage of human development can easily be discerned as the age of responsibility. The development of what psychologists have called "moral thought" is a long and gradual process. There are many gray areas between immaturity and moral responsibility in which, as every parent knows, it is difficult to decide whether youngsters should be allowed to make their own decisions or be held fully responsible for their mistakes. But the existence of this gray area does not undermine our suggested limitation on the term "indoctrination." We should say only that, in general, indoctrination becomes a concern and needs to be avoided precisely as autonomous or mature decision-making develops and needs to be encouraged. Understandably, this will be a gradual process over a number of years.

In attempting to develop acceptable criteria for moral education, therefore, we must be well aware of this large gray area in which decisions about educational practice will have to be made without absolute certainty. In our approach we will attempt to clarify that end of the scale on which the development of mature decision-making is assumed; we shall attempt to clarify what constitutes indoctrination and to develop criteria for avoiding it. If we are able to guard effectively against indoctrination at this level, we might then attempt to expand our efforts into the gray area of developing maturity with some assurance that our aim is ultimately one of education without indoctrination.[4]

We are fully aware that this stand on the training of young children may leave the criteria proposed here for the avoidance of indoctrination open to misuse. Teachers who do wish to continue indoctrinating their students might claim that their pupils, whether in first grade, high school, or college, are not old enough to reason for themselves. We believe that such an assumption cannot be justified beyond the first few years of formal education. This question, however, is a psychological one and open to a different kind of debate. It is a question of when the criteria of nonindoctrination which we suggest should be applied. Although we would argue for an early application of these criteria and would eagerly dispute those who blatantly indoctrinate on the assumption that young people cannot think for themselves, our task here is to develop a coherent idea of what is and what is not indoctrination in education beyond the early childhood stage. Perhaps if our criteria are clear and sound, we will be in a better position to decide when they ought to be applied.

## CONCEPTS OF INDOCTRINATION

Recent discussion of the nature of indoctrination has centered around two basic interpretations.[5] On the one hand, indoctrination is taken to be the inculcation of any set of beliefs when the foundation of, or evidence for, those beliefs is not open to public scrutiny.[6] The central idea here is that the *content* of the subject taught is an established doctrine, a value orientation, or a world view resting upon certain basic assumptions for which no rational justification exists. It is thus the doctrinal nature of the content of the subject that turns education into indoctrination. If one is teaching as the truth a body of knowledge or opinion which rests ultimately only upon unfounded assumptions, he is indoctrinating. Or, conversely, one can avoid indoctrination by teaching only what can be rationally justified as credible knowledge.

The major difficulty with this view is that it is not always possible to decide whether a certain set of beliefs is well founded and rationally credible or not. Capitalists and Communists, Christians and Buddhists would be likely to insist with equal vigor that their basic beliefs are in fact quite rational. And without an independent criterion of rational truth (and philosophers have never really found one), who is to say what is and what is not indoctrination? Anyone who believes his own opinions to be thoroughly rational would be justified in condemning any contrary set of beliefs as indoctrination in the purely prejudicial sense to which we objected.

Opposed to this "content" view is the "intention" theory, according to which the indoctrinator demands acceptance of the beliefs he is attempting to inculcate while refusing to permit those beliefs to be criticized.[7] In this case indoctrination is a matter of the way a subject is taught rather than a question of the rationality of the content. A person can thus be said to be indoctrinated if the instruction he is given persuades him to believe or accept what he is taught but does not permit (or sufficiently encourage) him to question the evidence or rationale behind it. Or, again conversely, indoctrination can be avoided by seeing to it that students freely consider the pros and cons of any belief or theory.

There are, however, serious objections to this understanding of indoctrination as well. First, a logical point: if the teacher said to be indoctrinating must *intend* that his students accept certain beliefs uncritically, then any teacher who did not actually intend this could not, by definition, be said to be indoctrinating. However, since we do commonly say that certain educational efforts constitute indoctrination, in spite of the teacher's intent, the concept of indoctrination must refer to something more. In terms of the intention theory the notion of unintentional indoctrination would be a logical contradiction, but it is really quite acceptable usage.

But the intention analysis of indoctrination also runs into much more practical difficulty. In the teaching of some subjects it is not expected that students learn to question what they are taught. The language teacher, for example, is not expected to encourage youngsters to question or criticize the forms of Latin verbs, nor should the mathematics teacher promote only a tentative acceptance of the multiplication table. In most subjects, for that matter, there is a standard body of knowledge accepted on "good authority" which is harmlessly taught as unquestioned truth prior to the effort to develop critical intellectual inquiry in students. An initial educational effort at the uncritical acceptance of knowledge of this sort should hardly be called indoctrination just because the teacher does not *intend* his students to consider the pros and cons of it.

The advocate of the intention theory of indoctrination might respond to this criticism, however, by insisting that if the content of the subject is not something that is seriously contested, one need not worry about students developing critical attitudes. If there are no real alternatives (one cannot really make up his own Latin verbs), there is nothing for students to be intellectually critical about.

But this response is not sufficient because it leaves open the question of who is to decide whether a subject is contested or not. Are there alternative views worthy of attention? This may seem a minor point, but it brings to light the inadequacy of the intention theory of indoctrination. The teacher, who has himself been indoctrinated with the prejudices of his society and lives and works in a society where few are conscious of the force of the alternatives, may not be concerned with his students' uncritical acceptance of what he believes he is teaching on "good authority."

This practical difficulty generated by the understanding of indoctrination as a matter of the educator's intention is thus not really much different from the difficulty which besets the "content" theory. On both views, as it turns out, teachers who are themselves indoctrinated, in the sense of not being open-minded about their subjects, might well insist that they have no intention of indoctrinating others because the beliefs they are teaching are commonly accepted on "good authority." If we tell teachers that they are indoctrinating their students, we must also tell them when the subject matter gives students the right to exercise their own judgment.[8]

## AN EMPIRICAL CRITERION

Perhaps we should not so easily assume that an adequate criterion by which to judge the content of a subject cannot be found. The real difficulty with the content approach, as it was first expressed by John Wilson, was its assumption that the necessary criterion for judging the content of an educational program must be a rational demonstration of its justifiability or credibility.[9] It must certainly be admitted that the wide philosophical disagreement which continues to exist over the nature of "rational demonstration" would make a neutral and independent criterion of this sort unobtainable, but it is not at all clear that such a rational demonstration is necessary. Would it not be better, in fact, to adopt a criterion that would refer to the current state of knowledge within a given field than to attempt to rely upon a purely rational judgment. One could then say that whenever a significant amount of disagreement exists—and this would be determined not logically but by an analysis of the different views people actually hold—teaching a particular set of beliefs or doctrines as necessarily "true" would be indoctrinating. The disputed logical or rational criterion would thus be replaced with one upon which at least some fairly rough empirical judgment could be made, a judgment as to whether disagreement with the doctrines in question actually exists or not among people knowledgeable in the field.

Such an empirical criterion would avoid the difficulties faced by both the content and the intention understandings of indoctrination. The degree of serious contrary opinion to a doctrine being presented would not be left to the teacher's or anyone else's judgment of what is rational; it could be determined by an actual survey of the subject in question. Thus the teacher who is himself indoctrinated could not escape the charge of indoctrination by insisting that he is only teaching the truth. No one would need to make a rational case against what the indoctrinator is teaching (a case which the teacher would not be likely to accept anyway). The mere fact that a significant group of other people actually do hold a contrary opinion —in short, that he is not dealing with an uncontested body of knowledge— would be sufficient evidence against the erring teacher. Should he respond that he is unaware of this contrary opinion, one could then admit the integrity of the teacher's intention but insist that he is unintentionally indoctrinating and nonetheless responsible for his own lack of knowledge of the subject, that is, for not knowing of the contrary opinion. Finally it might be noted that on the proposed empirical criterion the teaching of those subjects such as languages and mathematics, which are now taught in part by methods of direct inculcation, would escape criticism because in these subjects there is no significant disagreement among competent people in the field. The charge of indoctrination could not, therefore, be brought against teachers of these subjects.[10]

It might help, at this point, to formulate this notion of an empirical criterion of educational content into a definite principle. We shall state it in a negative form as a *criterion of nonindoctrination*. Stating the principle in this form is similar to efforts to establish criteria in many other fields; for instance, it is easier to develop a law defining what is prohibited than it is to formulate a law stating what is allowed. The thrust of our effort is toward establishing a criterion of nonindoctrination because we feel this to be the best approach to the problem both theoretically and practically. Therefore, although we shall say later that this is only a special case of a more general principle, we might state an initial criterion of non-indoctrination as follows: one cannot be said to be indoctrinating if he is teaching as true knowledge doctrines which are unobjectionable by general mutual consent determined by an analysis of informed opinion. Or, to put it more briefly, indoctrination can be avoided if the content is universally unobjectionable.

Four possible criticisms of this criterion will be considered briefly before moving on. First, it is certainly obvious that this criterion would cover very little of the content necessary for an adequate education in modern society. It actually reduces the content of education to such a small core of knowledge that education on this basis, while perhaps avoiding indoctrination, would be severely limited. To this we say that the criterion is not intended to cover much; it is only the first step toward an adequate and more comprehensive principle.

Second, and more important, it might be pointed out that universal mutual consent is not always easy to determine; deciding what is and what is not universally acceptable itself may involve serious dispute. This is certainly true, but it is a difficulty which must be accepted as a part of the task of education. The criterion admittedly places upon the educator (and upon his allies in the academic disciplines who bear equal responsibility for the development of educational materials) the responsibility of having a relatively thorough knowledge of the subject or content of educational programs. Actually having this fundamental knowledge, however, is one of the best ultimate safeguards against indoctrination: the teacher who truly recognizes the merits of different views of the same subject is not likely to be one who indoctrinates his students into any single opinion.

Third, it might be noted that even where the doctrinal content of an educational program is universally unobjectionable, the teacher may still present it in a way which tends to close students' minds—not to actual alternative opinions, because there are none if the content has passed the criterion—but to the possibility of future revision of what is currently accepted. Such teaching would indeed be objectionable, but like early childhood training which inhibits later development it is not necessarily a question of indoctrination. What is objectionable in this sort of teaching is the failure to get students to see the rationale of the subject rather than the actual misrepresentation of the truth of the doctrines being taught.

And finally, to ward off a possible philosophical objection, it ought to be mentioned that the appeal to universal mutual agreement or public consensus as a criterion for nonindoctrination does not imply in any way a criterion for human knowledge itself. Indeed, mutual agreement was long ago discredited as an epistemological criterion. Accordingly, the content approach to indoctrination runs into difficulty because it accepts the challenge of finding a criterion of nonindoctrination as an epistemological question and does not establish a universally credible criterion of rational justification. We do not admit, however, that the challenge is an epistemological matter; we take it rather as an ethical question—a matter of justice or fairness in education. And so our criterion is proposed as an ethical not an epistemological theory. The principle formulated above is suggested only as a guide to education and implies that *what we teach* (not what we claim to know) ought fairly or justly to reflect the knowledge situation *as it is*. This thesis thus supposes no epistemological basis; it is, rather, a corollary of a moral principle of justice or fairness.

## AN ANALYTICAL DEFINITION

The criterion formulated above is admittedly a rather limited principle. But before attempting to expand it, we must point out that we have come to see the concept of indoctrination in a new light. In particular, we have found that both the content and intention theories faced the same problem: one must make some judgment about the subject matter of education in order to say whether indoctrination is taking place or not. This has led us to suspect that there is really a closer relationship between these two understandings of indoctrination than was initially apparent. The truth of the matter may well be (as has been sometimes, but not very clearly, suggested in the literature on the subject) that the concept of indoctrination is a mixed notion involving both the content of the subject and the aims or intentions of the educator. The reason why indoctrination cannot be defined successfully in terms of either content or intention alone is that it is really a matter of the *communication* of knowledge and thus rests both on the nature of the knowledge involved and on the way in which that knowledge is transmitted. An adequate definition will therefore have to include considerations of both knowledge and transmission.

First we might look again at the knowledge aspect. The content view is inadequate because it is impossible to establish an impersonal or objective criterion of rational justification. What has often been neglected in the discussion of this point, however, is the fact that human knowledge does not simply come in propositions which are either true or false; they cannot be said to be simply "well-founded" or "ill-founded" belief. Human knowledge comes in all degrees and types of credibility, as many recent philosophers have taken pains to show. We "know" some things, but we only "believe" others; we are "relatively sure" about some things or are "absolutely certain" about others. We say that we "think," we "suspect," we "trust," and with a variety of phrases such as these we indicate the quality or form of the credibility of our beliefs. In normal discussion the terms we choose and the qualifying phrases we employ add what might be called credibility indicators to the statements we are making. Seldom, if ever, are we dealing with knowledge situations in which absolutely true or false statements are appropriate.

In the light of this understanding of the human knowledge situation indoctrination may be considered to depend not merely upon the representation of some belief as true when it is ill-founded but upon a misrepresentation *of whatever degree or type* of the credibility a belief or doctrine ought to have. One is indoctrinating when one conveys the impression that a certain statement has a credibility which, by public account (and here we can again employ our empirical criterion), it does not have. This would seem to be what was implied in Mr. Wilson's remark that "we must grade our teaching to fit the logical status of the beliefs which we are putting forward,"[11] except that for his suggestion of a "logical" criterion we would now employ an empirical measure.[12]

This understanding of the knowledge situation leads directly to consideration of the transmission of knowledge in teaching and to the question of the intent of the educator. One important insight of the intention theory is its recognition that indoctrination closes the student's mind to any criticism of the doctrine imparted. This consequence may be intentional or unintentional, but it is produced when the credibility of the doctrine is misrepresented. However, since credibility indicators are not always made explicit in normal discussion or in teaching but often depend only on the choice of words (as exemplified above) or even upon the nonverbal aspects of communication, it is very easy for a teacher to imply a higher (or lower) degree or kind of credibility than is actually (on public account) warranted. So a great deal depends upon the way subjects are taught because of the unofficial or tacit cues to credibility that are given. The truth of the intention theory is that indoctrination does depend upon communication—so much so that a teacher who pays serious attention to the credibility he is attributing to his subject is unlikely to be guilty of indoctrinating his students. If he actually wants his students to think for themselves, he need only take care not to misrepresent the credibility of his subject.

In defining indoctrination, therefore, we must include references, on the one hand, to the human knowledge situation with its wide range of credibility indicators and, on the other, to the accurate communication of knowledge. Indoctrination might then be defined as a misrepresentation of the credibility of the subject being taught or as communicating or imparting knowledge without fairly or accurately indicating its credibility. In both cases, of course, the credibility of the facts or theories professed would have to be determined by analysis of the knowledge situation as it is, that is, by the empirical criterion mentioned previously.

This definition of "indoctrination" is proposed not as a dictionary definition; it is an analytical one. We said earlier that we accepted the common meaning of indoctrination as education of which one disapproves, because it thwarts, hinders, or prevents people from exercising their own judgment. The purpose of an analytical or technical definition is to make the essence of the matter more precise, in this case for specific educational purposes. We are speaking theoretically, then, when we propose that the essence of indoctrination is a misrepresentation of the credibility of a subject.

## A GENERAL PRINCIPLE

The train of thought of this essay has led in two slightly different directions which we now wish to draw together. We began by establishing an empirical measure or criterion of the content of education by which the charge of indoctrination could be avoided. This criterion amounted to an assertion that, where there is no contrary opinion (as measured by a study of actual opinions on the doctrine in question), education can proceed without risk of indoctrination. An educator cannot be said to be indoctrinating if there is literally no objection to what he is teaching. He can, of course, still teach in a way that tends to close students' minds to the possibility of later revision. There is certainly much that is educationally wrong with this, but in the absence of any widely accepted alternatives, it may be best to avoid using the term indoctrination for this form of miseducation, just as it is best to avoid using the term for the training given in early childhood. Education can go wrong in many ways, but we need not try to make the term indoctrination cover all of them. At any rate, by the substitution of an actual study of the existing opinions on doctrinal content for the employment of so-called "rational" criteria which proved to be unavailable anyway, we were able to develop a rule of nonindoctrination which covered a small part of the problem: where there is universal mutual agreement on a doctrine, it can be taught without risk of indoctrination.

Returning to the question of definition, we can view the notion of misrepresenting the credibility of human knowledge as the essence of the concept of indoctrination: (1) if credibility is understood to cover a wide range of beliefs and attitudes rather than a simple true-false dichotomy, and (2) if misrepresentation is judged by an empirical survey of existing opinions. This definition fits our initial criterion: the reason educators cannot be guilty of indoctrination in cases where the doctrinal content of education is universally accepted is that in communicating such doctrines there is no risk of their misrepresenting the credibility of the subject.

This understanding of the essence of the concept now permits us to return to the question of education in those areas in which there is no universal agreement on the content. We turn, therefore, from the question of definition back to the effort to formulate a criterion of nonindoctrination, this time a general one, which will apply to all knowledge rather than only to doctrines which are acceptable by universal agreement.

If indoctrination consists of misrepresenting the credibility of the doctrines one is teaching, it can be avoided by seeing to it that credibility is accurately represented according to the present state of human knowledge. And a fair representation of the credibility of any single doctrine is achieved only when the claims of all widely held alternative opinions are presented fairly. What this means in practice, then, is that indoctrination can only be avoided if students are presented with the existing alternative beliefs on a somewhat equal basis according to the support for various positions within the academic discipline in question. The empirical criterion developed earlier can thus be expanded into a more general form which covers doctrinal content of subjects on which mutual agreement is unobtainable: *indoctrination can be avoided if equitable consideration is given to existing alternatives.*

This criterion actually includes the area covered by our first formula, since giving equal consideration to alternatives implies that if none exist (that is, by mutual consent), one need not worry about indoctrination. Teachers ought to be concerned with the degree of support that actually exists for the content of their teaching, and, of course, they ought to be concerned that education does not in other ways thwart the student's imagination. But the notion giving equal consideration to alternatives would certainly allow the direct teaching of doctrines as accepted truths where no alternatives exist. Thus, we are really working with two forms of the same criterion, both of which are based upon the notion that the knowledge situation should be represented fairly. For practical purposes, however, it is just as well to keep this principle in two forms. *Indoctrination can be avoided in either of two ways: (1) by assuring oneself of universal mutual consent on the doctrines taught, or (2) by giving equal consideration to existing alternatives where mutual agreement does not exist.*

While it is often helpful to have criteria or principles such as these at hand, such guidelines require intelligent application. We cannot leave the issue, therefore, without a few words of interpretation. First, these criteria of nonindoctrination will not provide an immediate or obvious solution to every problem. Even where they may be applied clearly, there is room for serious dispute over the existence of significant alternatives or mutual agreement. Such disputes will have to be settled within the fields of knowledge in question and by people who are reasonably competent in those fields. However, judgments of the significance of alternatives and of mutual agreement must be based on the actual range of current opinion on a subject rather than on the rational credibility of any single view.

Second, on a more practical level it might be asked whether absolutely every alternative must be presented in order for indoctrination to be avoided. For example, it would hardly seem justified in a science course to give equal time to the alternative proposed by the Flat Earth Society or in a literature course to consider every theory of literary criticism that has ever been formulated. A partial answer to this question can be given by reference to our definition. The important thing is to avoid misrepresenting the credibility of a doctrine. In subjects where there are many different opinions, misrepresentation of the credibility of a doctrine can be avoided by the presentation of *some* rather than *all* of the alternatives. Once the student recognizes the merits of some alternative claims, his mind is at least open to these considerations, and the credibility of the doctrine in question is not unduly misrepresented. It may be better, in fact, to present well only a few alternatives than to study the whole range superficially. Moreover, a less than adequate presentation of a significant alternative may serve to close students' minds to its real viability and thus increase the danger of indoctrination. The best brainwashing, it is often said, includes a rehearsal of the nature and faults of views opposed to the desired belief.

In the presentation of some rather than all other views the question of which positions to choose as representative becomes important. It would not suffice merely to present *any* other views, however unattractive, and then claim that this criterion has been satisfied. Plutocracy and theocracy are alternatives to democracy as forms of government, but they would hardly be attractive. One is not seriously avoiding indoctrination unless he presents a viable and attractive alternative, if there is one; the major alternatives certainly cannot be neglected. Again, this is a matter of the field of knowledge in question; our criterion will not settle all such disputes without reference to the knowledge situation as it exists in the various disciplines.

Another consequence of the principle of equal consideration as presented here is that different approaches are necessary for different subjects. Mathematical propositions, for example, can be expressed with a nearly absolute degree of certainty. The laws of physics are also established to a high degree of certainty. In history and economics knowledge is often spoken of as a matter of theory, and this is even more true in psychology and sociology. In the teaching of social and political philosophy at the level of basic theory (for example, comparative social and political systems), notions of "right" and "wrong" naturally give way to an evaluation of the pros and cons of the alternatives. In other subjects such as literature and art it seems somewhat inappropriate to speak about the "certainty" of human knowledge at all. Literature and art do have their factual sides (it is a fact, for example, that *Hamlet* was written before 1603), but in these subjects we normally look for "insight," "appreciation," "evaluation," or "understanding," without implying that it is at all a matter of certainty. Skills of interpretation, choice of interpretations, and other aspects of insight go well beyond factual matters and are normally expressed in language to which guarantees are not attached.

On the basis of this principle, then, we suggest that one can begin to consider education in a number of important subjects such as moral decision-making, politics, and perhaps even religion which in the past have been neglected or eliminated from the curriculum because of possible offense to the values and beliefs that people hold. The general principle of giving equal consideration to alternative views requires that major positions be presented with fairness and that the whole of the knowledge situation not be misrepresented. This means that the values and beliefs which people hold ought to be presented as values and beliefs—nothing more, but certainly nothing less. Political, moral, and religious beliefs hold an important place in men's lives and constitute the basis of their lifestyles and their day-to-day decisions: this must be emphasized. The fair presentation of alternatives would require that the respectability of various value orientations be admitted. If one religious faith, to take a difficult example, is not presented fairly by comparison with others, the educator is as much at fault for misrepresenting his subject as he would be in any other field. But it must also be said that if certain religious believers want their particular faith presented as "the truth" rather than as one of a number of alternatives, then it is *they*, and not the educators, who are proposing indoctrination.

The conclusion we draw is that although it is not always easy to identify indoctrination or to eliminate it from education, the adoption of a principle of equality along with a realistic evaluation of the nature of human knowledge in various subjects would work toward that goal. Inasmuch as our criteria are offered as principles or maxims, it might well be said that education without indoctrination is possible not as a definite attainment but rather as an ideal toward which progress can be made, rather like love between individuals or justice in society. As education is itself always something of an ideal, something to which the educator aspires, avoiding indoctrination is also a continual task or objective. Any principle which helps in this direction must be applied repeatedly as human knowledge changes and as social attitudes evolve. There can be no hard and fast determination, only an operational principle, but indoctrination can increasingly be avoided to the extent that educators, and the society whose representatives they are, are willing to make a continual effort to avoid it.

## NOTES

1. I. A. Snook, *Concepts of Indoctrination* (London: Routledge and Kegan Paul, 1972), p. 9.

2. Snook, *Concepts of Indoctrination,* p. 49.

3. R. M. Hare, "Adolescents into Adults," in *Aims in Education,* ed. T. H. B. Hollins (Manchester, England: Manchester University Press, 1964), p. 52.

4. For the sake of clarity we might note that the terms "doctrine" (referring to the content or subject matter of an educational program) and "inculcate" (referring to the transmission of knowledge) are here used as neutral or nonpejorative terms.

5. Although this section may serve to introduce readers to the recent debate over the nature of indoctrination, it is not intended as a comprehensive account. A number of other approaches have been suggested of which two, the "consequence" and the "method" theories, are mentioned in footnote 8.

6. John Wilson, "Education and Indoctrination," in *Aims in Education,* ed. T. H. B. Hollins (Manchester, England: Manchester University Press, 1964), pp. 24-46.

7. Hare, "Adolescents into Adults," pp. 47-70.

8. The "method" view of indoctrination (see W. Moore, "Indoctrination as a Normative Conception," *Studies in Philosophy and Education* 4 [Summer 1966]) and the "consequences" view (see T. F. Green, "A Typology of the Teaching Concept," *Studies in Philosophy and Education* 3 [Winter 1964-65]) can only be considered separate theories from the intention theory (often called also an "aim" theory) if one can effectively analyze educational methods or consequences apart from educational aims or intentions. We take it, however, that an educator *intends* the *consequences* of his *methods.* This may be a bit optimistic in practice, but to assume otherwise in theory is to suppose that education is not a rational enterprise. Methods which in effect indoctrinate without any such intent on the part of the educator are, in the first place, wrong as methods since they do not promote the educator's actual aims. Second, of course, they are wrong as indoctrination. And, similarly, unintentional indoctrination as a consequence of an educational program is wrong primarily because it is unintentional. We do not believe, therefore, that means (methods) and ends (consequences) are separable in any analysis of the process of education. Neither, furthermore, can be considered apart from an analysis of the intent, purpose, or aim of education. The real problem is how to avoid indoctrination in one's aims.

9. A view he later modified somewhat; see John Wilson, "Comments on Flew's 'What is Indoctrination?'" *Studies in Philosophy and Education* 4 (Summer 1966).

10. If carried further, this criterion could be shown to depend on the informal criteria of concept formation and credibility which exist in the various fields of human knowledge. For a comprehensive exposition on this point see S. Toulmin, *Human Understanding* (Oxford: Oxford University Press, 1972).

11. B. S. Crittenden, "Teaching, Educating, and Indoctrinating," *Educational*

*Theory* 18 (Summer 1968), pp. 28-29.

12. Something like this was hinted at by Professor Flew (see Anthony Flew, "What is Indoctrination?" *Studies in Philosophy and Education* 4 [Spring 1966]), but his notion of "logical geography" was obscured almost before it was explained by his apparent (and unconvincing) opinion that religious beliefs can never, in any way, be taught without indoctrinating, an opinion which seems utterly to ignore the distinction between teaching people *to believe* something and teaching people *about* something.

# 3

# An Integrated Approach

Setting the stage for our proposal has required something more than a brief introduction to the topic. We have attempted, first of all, to outline in a general way what we consider to be the moral domain, and we have tried to say why we believe education in this area is in need of direct attention. Second, we have also had to take a serious look at the question of how such education can be kept free of indoctrination, since it is especially important that we enter this domain with a clear idea of what we should and what we should not attempt to do educationally. Our approach to moral education has, at almost every turn, been guided by the principles of nonindoctrination we have just established, and we suggest that these considerations can provide a strong foundation both for the moral education teacher, who naturally wishes to develop a secure sense of what he is doing, and for school authorities, both professional and elected, who have the ultimate responsibility for giving an account of the nature and aims of education in this new field. At any rate, having adopted these guidelines, we can now attempt to outline our own perspective. However, our approach is related to recent research projects and proposals in the field, so it might be helpful just to mention some of the current efforts from which we have profited.

## BACKGROUND

The first contemporary attempt to develop a distinct program for moral education was organized by John Wilson, who was from 1965 until 1973 director of the Farmingon Trust Research Unit in Oxford, England. Although he attempted to give full consideration to the psychological and social aspects of the subject, Mr. Wilson's philosophical orientation clearly dominated his approach. While this approach has often been criticized for its excessive philosophical or rational emphasis, from our point of view it sets an important precedent. Since nearly all of the recent discussion of moral education in the United States springs from psychological research, Wilson's early effort now stands as a good example of a humanistic perspective in the field—a perspective we are seeking to restore.

The essence of Mr. Wilson's approach is that moral education should consist not in the teaching of any specific set of moral rules but in communicating a rational method which an individual can use to develop his own moral principles. Basically, this rational method is the product of Wilson's determination of the necessary components of moral thought. The component factors are then treated as specific skills, abilities, and attitudes which can be developed through appropriate educational techniques. The program itself centers upon four of these basic skills: (1) showing concern for other people as equals, (2) awareness of other people's feelings and emotions, (3) knowledge of the facts relevant to moral decisions, and (4) the ability to act upon one's own decisions. Through education in these skills, abilities, and attitudes, as Mr. Wilson sees it, young people can be equipped to think morally without being indoctrinated in any particular moral code. As he states his objective, "We are not primarily out to impart any specific *content*, but to give other people facility in a method."[1] The components of moral thought "are not the peculiar property of any particular faith, creed, set of moral values or partisan beliefs, but qualities and rules of procedure which define what it is to be reasonable or serious about morality."[2]

The value of this highly original effort can hardly be overestimated. For the first time it was suggested that principles and values be communicated to the young not by direct teaching, but by fostering the ability of young people to develop their own principles and to make their own decisions. In effect this proposal has put the whole notion of moral education on a new footing. Indeed, it is only on this basis that moral education can be undertaken in a free and pluralistic society. Mr. Wilson's proposal establishes the high standards that are needed in this field; its intent is clearly to avoid indoctrination, and at the same time it is a serious effort at education in the moral domain.

Departing somewhat from Mr. Wilson's focus of attention, a second effort in England has taken a more practical direction. The Schools Council Moral Education Curriculum Project, initiated in 1967, has recently produced a full set of materials for moral education on the middle and secondary school levels.[3] Beginning with a study of social and personal problems actually faced by young people, the members of this project attempted to isolate the areas of moral thought and action which are most important to students and thus most in need of educational attention. Their research, both in the investigative stage and in the development of teaching materials, was extensive; some twenty thousand youngsters and teachers were involved prior to the final publication of the program. Following the apparent implications of this research, the approach adopted was one of avoiding heavy reliance upon a philosophical theory of the nature of morality which might seem especially complicated and, therefore, irrelevant to young people. As a result the Schools Council's materials focus on the development of better social relations and concern for other people. In the first phase of the program, for example, a unit called "sensitivity" is designed "to improve people's ability to recognize their own and other's needs, interests, and feelings and to help them understand why they behave as they do," while another unit "puts the emphasis on improving boys' and girls' ability to predict the possible and probable consequences of action."[4] The second phase of the program moves the student's attention to the demands of society and the development of the individual's identity. It is concerned with the social norms and values which young people experience as social "pressures." In the final phase of the program, an attempt is made to expand the student's developing moral perspective to include social problems on a national and international scale. In effect the Schools Council's program is broadly humanistic and centers upon the single moral value of taking account of the interests of other people.

While the materials of this program can serve as an example of directing education to the needs and interests of students, it must be asked whether a program with such broad and general aims can ever get to the heart of the matter or not. In the early stages it does indeed center upon the development of specific skills and abilities (sensitivity to others and consideration of the consequences of actions), but by the second phase, with its emphasis on personal identity and then later on with its expansion to national and international issues, the program seems to lose its moral focus. It is surely a mistake to let the concept of morality, which we take to be a matter of decisions involving values and ideals, be transformed into questions of personal relations and social problems. These are indeed important areas for human development, and they are related to the moral domain in essential ways. But in our opinion the skills of interpersonal relations and the understanding of social issues are matters which ought to be treated educationally in their own right so that moral education can be free to concentrate upon the particular problem of evaluation and decision. Discussion of moral issues as it now occurs in classrooms is already so broad and general that it risks turning into nothing more than a common bull session. The task of moral education, as we see it, is to bring some order out of the normally confused and chaotic thinking in this domain, and we feel that this can better be accomplished by centering upon limited moral issues than by dealing with general social problems of international conflict.

In the United States concern for moral education has taken its lead from the field of cognitive psychology. A model of the stages of moral development constructed by Professor Lawrence Kohlberg at Harvard University has been generally confirmed through a number of research projects. Most recently he has entered into a combined effort with Professors Edwin Fenton and Barry Beyer at Carnegie-Mellon University for the development and testing of teaching methods and materials for social studies curricula. The method they propose is the classroom discussion of hypothetical moral dilemmas. According to Kohlberg's theory, this discussion will help to raise the level of the student's moral thought indirectly by revealing the inadequacies of his current stage and by presenting him with better modes.

Of course we cannot presume to judge what this project will have to offer when it is completed. We suspect, however, that its psychological orientation will produce the view that moral education is simply one indirect influence facilitating the cognitive stage of development and that the philosophical or humanistic understanding of the decision-making process has no special importance as a rational process. Moral growth may well involve the development of higher levels of cognitive stages, but we believe it can and should also be understood as the development of certain basic thought skills. His more recent efforts at moral philosophy notwithstanding, Kohlberg's approach to moral education remains psychologically exclusive in that it tends to reject the idea that any direct teaching of rational skills is at all appropriate.

However, Kohlberg's attempt to view the subject from his single perspective adds an important element to the total picture. Moral education needs a psychological foundation which is both firm in its research base and explicit enough to be of practical use. The Kohlberg model may have its problems, but it is, in our view, substantially sound as a general theory and sufficiently explicit to be of practical use to educators.

Our own proposal for moral education takes account of these efforts, though it does not rely too heavily on any one of them. Mr. Wilson's ground-breaking work has provided a model for the development of the philosophical analysis we shall present, although our approach is based upon a slightly different account of the concept of morality and a correspondingly different assessment of the skills of rational moral thought. Professor Kohlberg's research provides a working model of moral development in our approach, although we have at least one major reservation concerning his theory and some comments about its use. The program sponsored by the Schools Council has inspired us to develop an approach which is guided in a number of essential ways by educational theory, in particular by the principle of education without indoctrination. Our approach, therefore, is an integrative one which, we hope, incorporates the best of each of these orientations but does not rely too heavily on any single perspective. In contrast to the psychological orientation of most of the recent discussion of moral education in the United States, however, ours is a proposal which can easily be understood as a philosophical or humanistic model. While we would not reject this characterization, we hope it does not imply that we do not give due consideration to the psychology of moral development.

## A PHILOSOPHICAL ANALYSIS OF MORAL JUDGMENT

The first component of our proposal is a philosophical analysis of the concept of morality. We shall attempt to develop as clear a description as possible of precisely what constitutes a *moral* reason for action or a decision based upon *moral* considerations. A moral judgment, as we shall define it, is a decision which as a matter of principle commits an individual to a certain kind of action. Second, moral reasons for action are recognizable in that they take priority over other possible reasons and motives. The third and most important characteristic of a moral judgment is that the person who makes it must be willing to apply it impartially to all people; a moral action cannot be perfectly all right for one person but not for another if the circumstances are identical. And finally, the moral principles to which an individual commits himself normally constitute a more or less unified pattern of personal and social ideals.

At first sight this description of the nature of moral judgment may seem to be a rather minimal or low-key analysis. It may contain few of the concepts or ideas the reader would customarily associate with the term "moral," but we must keep in mind the requirements of our educational task: our goal is not to teach youngsters to hold any particular moral values or principles. Our objective is, rather, to teach young people what a moral value or a moral judgment is so that they can identify moral considerations when they meet them and become aware of the place of moral values in their own decision-making. The first step in moral education (logically, if not in practice) is to develop an awareness of such things as moral judgments, values, and principles. Discussion of specific moral values—justice, equality, the sanctity of life—will have little real effect on people who have no concept of a moral viewpoint.

A second educational objective drawn from our philosophical analysis is derived from the notion that in approving certain actions one must be prepared to have others act in that way and to live in a society where such actions are common. In developing the ability to make moral judgments, therefore, young people must be brought to consider some rather practical questions: Will they *always* act in the way they *now* propose? Are they satisfied with *all* of the consequences of their actions? Will they be happy to have others act in the same way? What kind of society will result if others regularly act in the way they suggest? From a philosophical perspective moral education must challenge people to consider the moral implications

of their decisions and actions. Our proposal assumes that moral development can be fostered if, like Socrates, we try to ask the right questions so
that young people acquire the habit of considering their actions more fully
in the light of moral consequences. The skills of moral thought which we
shall thus attempt to develop consist largely of the ability to pose such
questions for oneself with respect to one's own actions.

Our purpose, therefore, will not be to teach particular values as such
but only to develop a sense of the nature and purpose of value decisions.
What analytical philosophy has to offer to a program for moral education
is a description of what constitutes a genuine moral judgment. It tells us
the difference between good and poor moral reasoning, not the "right"
answers to moral problems. It tells us *how* we ought to think, not *what* we
ought to decide. Our proposal for moral education is based first of all on
the assumption that we can, through a Socratic method, induce students
to consider the morally relevant consequences of their decisions and
actions.

## A PSYCHOLOGICAL ACCOUNT OF MORAL DEVELOPMENT

Although philosophical analysis may tell us how we ought to think if
we want to take moral considerations into account, how people actually
think is another matter—a matter for psychological study. An effective
program for moral education must take account of this perspective as well.
We cannot expect youngsters to think as mature adults or even to accept
adult reasons for actions which they do not adequately comprehend. We
must first try to understand how youngsters think and then attempt to
promote growth toward the more mature pattern of moral thought described by the philosopher. If analytical philosophy provides a description
of the goal or aim of moral education, we still need a psychology of moral
development to provide an analysis of the path to that goal.

While there certainly has been little agreement among psychologists
on the matter of moral development, recent research in one psychological
school of thought has produced results which are relevant to our
educational task. The essence of the cognitive development theory, initiated by Jean Piaget and recently advanced by Professor Kohlberg, is the
supposition that moral thought develops through a definite series of
stages, phases, or modes, each of which forms a relatively coherent pattern
for making moral decisions. Thus, during infancy and early childhood the

youngster is basically egocentric; he sees the world in terms of how it affects his welfare personally and makes his decisions on the basis of personal pleasure or reward. Later in childhood and into adolescence he begins to see the world more in terms of its social or legal order, and he bases his decisions on whether an action is approved or condemned by his social reference group or by the unofficial norms of his family, by his religion, or by civil law. At yet a later stage the young person begins to develop or adopt his own personal values and principles which then constitute the basis of his moral decisions and his judgments of others. A more detailed description of this psychological development will be offered later; at this point we wish only to indicate the nature of the psychological contribution to our proposal. Moral education is in part a matter of presenting youngsters with examples of moral reasoning at a higher level so that their current modes of thought will be challenged and will give way to a more mature stage. The goal of this process of growth, facilitated, we hope, by education, is the level at which the psychological description of moral thought and the philosophical analysis of moral judgment converge—the stage of mature moral thought.

However, the cognitive aspect of man's moral nature is not the only aspect of moral development that deserves educational and psychological attention. The ability to think clearly about moral issues and to carry moral decisions into action depends upon other factors such as personal development, social adjustment, and interpersonal relations. Although we are convinced that moral education should concentrate on decision-making and, in general, consider questions of personal development and human relations as separate educational concerns, the relationship of moral development to personal growth is indeed a close one and cannot be neglected. These concerns will become especially important when we begin to consider the classroom setting or atmosphere for moral education. We shall, therefore, give some attention to the insight of personality theory, especially to the views of Carl Rogers, centering on the implication of these insights for the creation of a classroom atmosphere in which moral growth can be facilitated. The moral education classroom, we contend, must not be viewed as a center for moral instruction (that is, for learning maxims, rules, or the "right" answers to problems) or for moral influence (that is, a series of good examples); it must be considered an environment in which youngsters can learn to think morally for themselves. Students will have to be presented with opportunities for developing the necessary skills of moral thought and will have to be challenged and attracted by moral reasoning that is a bit more mature than their own.

When we conceive of the classroom as an environment for moral growth, however, we must also think of the educator as a person who establishes the environment and guides or facilitates interaction within it rather than as an instructor or even a "teacher" in the narrower sense of that term. This environment should be conducive to the discussion of moral issues and to the playing out of moral situations in role play or educational games. The teacher's responsibility is to help students clarify their own thoughts and feelings, to challenge students to consider the full consequences of their decisions in the light of personal and social values, and to confront them with new considerations and perspectives. On the whole, moral education is a developmental process rather than a subject which can be directly taught, although later we shall consider the more or less direct teaching of some of the necessary rational skills.

## FROM THEORY TO PRACTICE

We shall have, then, two perspectives on the moral domain: a philosophical analysis of the nature of moral judgment and a psychological account of the stages of moral development. Our final task will be to elaborate an educational theory that will integrate these two perspectives as well as satisfy our criterion of nonindoctrination.

What kind of classroom and teaching methods will be necessary to achieve our goal of moral sensitivity and growth? The classroom atmosphere for moral education must be both open and real. It must be open in the sense that students are encouraged and supported in developing their own thinking rather than being presented with idealized "right" thought patterns or the "correct" answers. The challenge of being confronted by moral issues and better modes of thought can be effective only in an open environment. The classroom must be real in the sense of dealing with genuine issues—"real life" situations with many facets, many relevant considerations, and, in all likelihood, no clear answers. To make the environment real, however, the teacher must be honest with his students. He must listen to their opinions with respect and avoid compelling the discussion toward his own preconceived conclusion. The teacher will, of course, have his own moral opinions, and he must be free to share them honestly while being careful not to present them as the "right" answers. If students feel that they are supposed to be learning moral thinking from someone else rather than developing their own thought, they will quickly learn how to say the right things for class purposes; such "exercises" will have little positive effect on the way students actually make decisions for themselves.

In the final chapters of this book we shall propose definite methods by which moral development can be facilitated. One educational strategy will be an adaptation of the age-old, but rarely employed, case study method. The particular emphasis we shall propose in the use of this technique is currently advocated by psychologically oriented moral education theorists and can be adapted to the philosophical objectives of our approach.

A second teaching strategy will be a particular kind of discussion of moral concepts and principles directed toward the development of the skills of moral thought. Through a comparison of various decisions and their consequences and through an analysis of the nature of some of the more common moral concepts people employ, students can be brought to pose for themselves the kinds of questions which constitute a more mature pattern of moral reasoning. And finally, we shall discuss the use of educational games and simulations in moral education, a strategy which is still in a developing state but is extremely impressive in its effectiveness.

Our plan for moral education, therefore, is the creation of a classroom environment of open discussion, interaction, and experience. However, at the same time we shall propose that it be a controlled environment in which the teacher employs the tools of both philosophical and psychological analysis and is guided by the principles of education without indoctrination. We do not expect, of course, to be able to answer all the questions one might have regarding moral education within the compass of this brief presentation. We hope only to provide a framework of basic principles, the fundamentals of an approach which might be used as the basis for a few initial and tentative steps toward education in this domain.

## NOTES

1. John Wilson, N. Williams, and B. Sugarman, *Introduction to Moral Education* (London: Penguin, 1968), p. 27.
2. John Wilson, *Practical Methods of Moral Education* (London: Heinemann Educational Books, 1972), p. 5.

3. P. McPhail, J. R. Ungoed-Thomas, and H. Chapman, *Moral Education in the Secondary School* (London: Longmans, 1972).

4. McPhail, Ungoed-Thomas and Chapman, *Moral Education in the Secondary School*, p. 100.

# Philosophical Analysis I:
# Principles and Priorities

## THE CONCEPT OF MORALITY—A GENERAL DEFINITION

The initial problem faced by any proposal for education in morality is to clarify the subject. In many respects this is the most complex aspect of the project, for moral philosophers have disagreed not only about specific moral principles and about the propriety of particular actions but also, and rather sharply, about exactly what a constitutes *moral* judgment or a *moral* reason. Indeed, in recent years moral philosophy has centered almost entirely on the nature of moral judgment rather than on the propriety of particular courses of action. Nevertheless, if we propose to develop a coherent and effective program for education in this domain, we must attempt to construct a definition of morality which will prove reasonably acceptable to people who hold different moral perspectives or theories.

That moral philosophers themselves disagree even about the nature of morality is not peculiar to our topic. Literary critics disagree about the nature of poetry, and art critics puzzle over what is and what is not a work of art. Disputes about the nature of subject matter are also common among historians and natural scientists, especially when it comes to deciding what ought to be taught at the secondary school level. In all fields some tolerable agreement about the nature of the subject is necessary for educational purposes; that is our aim here as well.

To begin with, it must be fully recognized that people hold different moral views. They disagree about the propriety of particular actions and about what is best for society as a whole. We cannot, therefore, take any single moral perspective or system of rules and establish it as the norm for moral education. This would constitute indoctrination of the worst sort. Our effort must concentrate on an account of the nature of morality which frankly admits of a very wide range of moral viewpoints and does justice to the essence of each. We need, in other words, a definition of morality which is itself somewhat neutral; this definition of what constitutes a moral decision must be sufficiently general to apply equally well to decisions made by people of quite different moral perspectives. It may seem odd to speak of a "morally neutral definition of morality," but that is exactly what is needed. To define morality by reference only to some particular kinds of moral decisions would be like defining poetry as "verses that rhyme" or "iambic pentameters." Such definitions would be misleading because they would exclude so much recognized poetry. Likewise, our definition of morality must cover everything that people normally recognize as moral decisions.

It follows from this that our description of the concept of morality cannot itself involve the presentation of any particular moral judgments or rules. Our analysis must be directed at the general nature of the subject, just as, for example, physics might be described as "the study of the properties of energy and matter." And just as this definition of physics does not include reference to any particular physical theories (Newton's law or Heisenberg's principle), so a definition of morality cannot include references to particular moral judgments (Hitler was evil) or moral rules (never tell a lie).

Finally, it must be admitted at the outset that since we are proposing a neutral definition of the subject—one acceptable to people of virtually all moral perspectives—we must allow our definition to be subject to the test of further discussion and examination. The ultimate justification of any proposal such as this can only be its actual acceptance by people of different moral points of view. In the end we shall have to rely upon some sort of agreement to get this program off the ground. We realize that our objective of a value-free definition of morality is a rather high ideal and success is a matter of degree rather than of clear attainment. There is, however, no justifiable way to proceed except to ask for mutual consent and hope that our own value orientation has not been overly intrusive. If anyone seriously objects to the general description of morality offered here, nothing can be done except for us to try to come to an agreement on some definition and to revise our educational proposal accordingly. In constructing a general definition, therefore, we are making a positive theoretical recommendation or proposal for which mutual assent, rather than logical proof, is the ultimate criterion.

## OUTLINE OF THE CONCEPT

There are undoubtedly many different ways of describing what morality is all about, but we suggest that the concept can be sufficiently described by reference to four basic characteristics:

1. A moral judgment is a decision which is, for the person who makes it, a matter of *principle* in that he commits himself to a certain type of action or sincerely recommends it to others.
2. Moral principles and the decisions related to them take *priority* over other motives or reasons for actions.
3. Moral principles are *universal;* they apply impartially to all.
4. A moral perspective may be regarded as the adoption of a framework of personal and social ideals which form a comprehensive view of one's own life and of the society in which one lives.

Obviously, such a brief definition cannot include all that should be said about moral thought. Nevertheless we believe that it will prove sufficient for our purpose; it is sufficiently neutral to be acceptable to people who hold different moral perspectives and yet sufficiently forceful to distinguish moral decisions and moral reasons from other reasons and motives for actions. In this chapter we will describe the first two of these points; the remaining two will be described in the following chapter.

## DECISIONS AND PRINCIPLES

Moral opinions and beliefs concern people's decisions about their actions. When someone says that it is wrong to steal or that it is good to help those in need, he is talking about things that people do or might do, and he is taking a position for or against such actions. What is characteristic of *moral* terms—terms such as "good" or "bad," "right" or "wrong" —is that they are all used to express opinions about actions. (They might well express more than this; we are saying here only that they express *at least* this.) When people use this language, they are actually formulating and giving their opinions, recommending certain actions, advising against others, and in general guiding human behavior. We may have many different reasons for what we say—for recommending some things and condemning others—but for all of them we are making decisions both for ourselves (if we are using these concepts in thinking about our own actions) and for others (if we use this language in arguing or discussing). As philosophers have often pointed out, this is what is implied in the dictionary definition of the term "good" as the most general term of commendation in the English language. The concepts and ideas of moral thought are, first of all, beliefs and opinions about human actions, both our own and others. This is not all that morality is; it involves other elements as well, but it is still important to realize that whatever the motives or reasons for moral opinions, they are either for or against the human actions about which we find it necessary to make decisions.

In speaking about this double function of guiding one's own action and recommending action for others, some recent philosophers have said that moral language is characteristically "prescriptive." A doctor gives a prescription to a sick patient, but really he is recommending or advising the patient to take a certain drug for the sake of his health, and he does this, we might say, according to the current *principles* of medical theory. Given a reluctant patient, he might even say, "If I were as sick as you, this is what I would take." And this is, indeed, exactly what goes on in our normal use of moral language; we are basically prescribing certain courses of action for ourselves (in deciding) and for others (in discussing). Thus, moral language and thought might all be called prescriptive in that they are essentially action-guiding.

It is because of this action-guiding function of moral thought and language that people often speak about moral principles. *A principle is a general recommendation for or against a certain kind of action in certain situations.* Whenever a person decides on a course of action (whatever his reasons might be), he is implying that in his opinion the course of action he recommends or follows is the one that ought to be taken in a certain kind of situation. If, for example, someone gives money to the Salvation Army or if he recommends this form of charity to others, he is at least tentatively committing himself to the idea that people should help the poor in this or some similar way, that is, that the poor ought to be helped rather than, say, put in jail. It can be said, then, that by making a decision a person is formulating or beginning to formulate a principle of action. Principles, in turn, might be thought of primarily as generalizations formed from a series of individual decisions. A decision implies a principle, the belief that in a particular situation the decision made and the action suggested is the best one. Thus, the relationship between making decisions and formulating principles is a reciprocal one; as Professor R. M. Hare has said, we are always setting precedents for ourselves.

We can, of course, speak about principles which would hardly be called moral principles, such as "When driving, always keep to the right" or "Third hand play high (in bridge)." But people also generally hold principles which are recognizably moral, even though of a sometimes relatively minor sort, such as "Only make promises you intend to keep" or "Help those in need or distress" or even "Be kind to animals." Whether a principle is a moral one or not depends upon factors we shall discuss later, but it can at least be said that morality involves principles of action or that moral actions are based upon decisions of principle. This does not mean that all such principles must be considered absolute or must never be broken, nor does it imply that people who hold moral principles necessarily act on them. It is only to say that moral actions are characteristically *principled* actions or actions consistent with general maxims.

Furthermore, to say that decisions are based upon principles does not at all imply that a principle must be previously and consciously adopted before a decision can be made—far from it. An actual decision is often only the beginning of the process through which a moral principle is developed. If one decides to do a certain thing in a given situation and it turns out that he is later satisfied with what he has done or convinced that it was the right thing to do, he is likely to choose the same alternative the next time he faces that particular issue or one reasonably like it. At this point we can say that he has begun to formulate a principle of action for himself. But decisions and principles can also be revised or even abandoned in the face of further experience. If a person does not like the results (perhaps some of them unforeseen) of his decision in a certain case or if he is convinced that for some reason he should have done otherwise, he is likely to try an alternative the next time. He is still formulating a principle for himself; only this time it is a negative one: "Don't try that again." It may in fact take a number of decisions and revisions before a person can be said to have established a principle, and even then conscientious men are not particularly criticized for changing their opinions if they do so responsibly.

Some people, of course, think of moral principles as *rules* of conduct and go on to speak about the whole of morality as a matter for action. There is certainly nothing wrong with thinking about morality in this way, especially if the notion of personal decision is emphasized so that one thinks primarily of drawing up the rules *for himself,* a code to live by, or whatever it might be called. Since we so often think of rules as laws or regulations laid down by an authority of some sort, this way of stating the concept seems to us to allow the whole field of moral thought to slip too easily into an authoritarian "Follow the rules" framework or to become only a list of "dos and don'ts." Once this happens, moral decisions all too easily get viewed only as a matter of following the dictates of one's parents, society, or church without really formulating one's own guidelines and beliefs. Since it is this sense of personal moral decision that we are trying to emphasize, we shall stay with terminology conducive to it and speak about moral principles, maxims, beliefs, ideals, and values, rather than about moral rules or moral law. We do not mean to imply that people ought to make up their own moral rules without the aid of parents, or religious, or cultural institutions. Moral education ought to be centered around a consideration of basic traditional values; however, each person is, in the end, his own moral agent, and his lifestyle is really his own choice. That is what morality is all about. Personal decision, for that matter, is an essential aspect of moral thought even if one does decide to follow closely the moral guidance of a religious community or a social peer group. One still has to choose to accept such guidance and can never escape responsibility for one's own actions by appealing to such "authorities." "He told me to do it" is an excuse that is used only by morally immature children.

While it might seem that very little is accomplished by simply pointing out that morality has to do with conscious personal decisions about actions, there is one particular sense in which this is a most important point, especially when we come to consider moral education. A great deal of confusion arises in the discussion of moral problems through the failure to recognize exactly what is and what is not human judgment, or, to put it another way, what is a matter of fact and what a matter of moral or personal opinion. In particular, we often fail to recognize the extent to which the way we look at the world and the society in which we live is already colored by the opinions of those around us, especially parents and close friends. All too often even the language we use implies approval or disapproval of certain actions or embodies a positive or negative attitude taken over unconsciously from the society around us.

Philosophers often speak, therefore, of a distinction between facts (a plain or neutral description of the world) and values (personal attitudes toward objects and actions). Some philosophers have insisted that to be clear about our moral thinking we must recognize that facts and values are two very different kinds of things, that the state of affairs is one thing and our opinion about it is another. There is good reason for this emphasis because it helps us to see exactly when decisions are being made. Other philosophers, however, have objected to drawing such a hard and fast distinction between facts and values, pointing out that many human values are as much a part of the world as sticks and stones: man values food because he needs it for sustenance. However, even if values are in this way implicit in the world around us, it is man who must discern and act upon these values, so without saying that either of these groups of philosophers is correct, we can recognize the great extent to which moral decisions are a matter of human choice.

This distinction can be helpful, however, when it is used as a procedural method in trying to analyze moral decisions. When considering a particular moral judgment, we might ask first, what exactly are the facts of the matter (as objectively as they can be stated) and, second, what are the values involved (even if they are "related" to general factual considerations). It is important, at any rate, not to let our moral choices be overridden by unconscious prejudices which may creep into our understanding of a problem by way of the emotional content of our common language. Prejudices are unfortunately built into our social structures and language, and they get in the way of moral thought by preventing people from even considering the possible alternatives. For example, if as a child one learns only the term "nigger" as a reference to black people, one's attitude toward members of other races becomes negative without his even realizing that he has any choice in the matter. It is nearly impossible to develop or adopt a trustworthy moral principle if one cannot even visualize the alternatives. For instance, in the novel *1984* people were prevented from holding opinions contrary to state teaching because they were forced to use a language which had no words for those opinions.

A first step in moral education, therefore, is to realize as fully as possible the realm of choice one actually has, and to do this we must try to get rid of our own prejudices. We may, of course, come to conclusions quite similar to those commonly held by people in our society, but that is quite different from holding an opinion merely because it is widespread. Realizing that we have made a decision for ourselves provides us with a more genuine moral perspective than simply seeing the world with the prejudices we inherit from family and friends, even if the opinion is the same.

Finally, we should note that there is certainly nothing sacred about our using the word "principles" to designate this aspect of moral thought. Others speak in much the same manner of moral beliefs, values, ideals, or opinions.

However, understanding in one way or another the nature of moral principles, values, or beliefs and recognizing that decisions about one's own actions ultimately constitute one's moral principles is really a very important aspect of the moral point of view. Morality is a matter of developing a reasonably consistent and coherent set of beliefs or principles which one is willing to stand by as his consciously adopted lifestyle. What people often do not realize is that *such a lifestyle is actually built step by step out of the decisions they make every day* and that it is the sum total of the principles that are implicit in their decisions. The development of a moral perspective is thus dependent upon constant attention to the long-range implications of one's own decisions and actions. When people fail to realize this, however, they are inclined just to drift along from decision to decision, sometimes wondering why their lives seem to have no aim or purpose and never recognizing that they are nevertheless establishing a lifestyle (such as it is). Of course, one can actively attempt to avoid adopting a moral perspective, but most often, rather than intending to be immoral, people simply fail to consider the long-range implications of their actions and thus fail to see the principles they are actually establishing for themselves. As one moral philosopher has said, "Eyes they have, but do not see; ears they have, but do not hear."

We will not pause at this juncture to consider the educational implications of the notion of morality as principled decision, but it might be
helpful to keep in mind two points for future reference. First, morality as
the development of a lifestyle is implicit in a person's decisions and actions
even when he does not think about what he is doing in any *conscious* sense.
Moral education, therefore, is in part a matter of *simply* (the idea is simple, perhaps not the practice) trying to get people to think about their decisions and actions, to consider the long-range consequences of their
actions and to develop the idea that they are actually determining their
own lifestyles for the future by what they now choose and do. The second
point is related to what we called the procedural method of separating
facts and values. The development of moral thought can be advanced, we
believe, by helping people to assess the *facts* of human life accurately and
thereby to look at decision situations more objectively. The ability to
separate fact and opinion can facilitate moral thought and discussion.

## THE PRIORITY OF MORAL PRINCIPLES

We have said that morality has to do with the decisions people make
to act in one way or another and that, in the long run, these decisions
imply and support principles which constitute a person's lifestyle or moral
perspective. But we have not said much about people's motives or reasons
for their decisions, or for the principles they hold. This is the subject of our
second point.[1]

People act as they do, of course, for many different reasons: they desire something, they are afraid of punishment or of what others might say
or think, they wish to help friends or resist enemies, or they are simply
angry, jealous, or bored. Not all of these motives or reasons for actions,
however, can be called moral reasons. This is not because some of them
are immoral but because they are not yet sufficiently well considered or
thought out to be called either moral or immoral. They might at this stage
be called nonmoral, though some may certainly develop into moral reasons. Moral reasons for actions are reasons which are rather well considered or evaluated in relation to the whole of one's own life and to the
society in which one lives. A morally acceptable action is one which is
judged *on the whole, or all things considered*, the best course of action.
Morality thus has to do not with the immediate reasons or motives one
might give for his actions but with one's *ultimate* reasons for acting—the

best or highest reasons one can give for his decisions.

We often act, of course, on the basis of our immediate feelings or opinions without thinking things out carefully. But this is mostly confined to trivial or less important matters; I do not need to have a moral reason for putting down my pen in the midst of writing this paragraph to get a cup of coffee. In speaking about the moral point of view, therefore, we are certainly not saying that one must ponder every step taken. However, one can also be at fault for treating a matter lightly when it deserves serious consideration. Matters which affect our own lives and the lives of others seriously and over a long period of time require the best consideration we can give them.

What characterizes moral reasons or motives in general, therefore, is not that they are reasons or motives of any certain kind but that they are, at least for the person who acts upon them, the final, highest, or ultimate reasons upon which he would act. To put this another way we might say that a moral act is one which is still considered best after all of the consequences of the various alternatives have been taken into account. This point about moral thought is nicely described in the following passage by Professor P. H. Nowell-Smith:

> A man's moral principles are "dominant" in the sense that he would not allow them to be over-ridden by any pro-attitude other than another moral principle. Thus a man may belong to many organizations and be allowed by the laws of his country to do something that he is not allowed to do by the rules of his trade union, profession or church. When a conflict of principles or loyalties arises he may wonder what he ought to do; but it is part of the force of the phrase "moral principle" that he cannot (logically) wonder what he ought to do if there is a moral principle on one side and not on the other. If I regard something as immoral, then, however trivial it may be and however great may be the non-moral advantages of doing it, I cannot debate with myself whether I ought to do it; and we discover what our own moral principles are very often by putting just this sort of question to ourselves.
>
> A similar limitation in the use of the phrase "moral principle" comes out in our attitude to compensation. A man will not lightly give up a moral principle; nor will he lightly give up anything else that he regards as valuable. But our attitude towards giving up a moral principle differs from all other cases. If a man has a picture that he values very highly he may reject a low price and be more inclined to part with it if the bid is raised. But if a man refuses a bribe of ten pounds [$25] and you offer him a hundred [$250], he might say: "You don't understand; it is not a question of how much;

doing that sort of thing is against my moral principles." Indeed he must say this, if it is really a matter of moral principle, unless he can manage to bring the acceptance of the offer under some other moral principle. It is for this reason that Napoleon's dictum that every man has his price sounds so cynical; it implies that no man has any moral principles.[2]

At this point it might be helpful to notice again that this understanding of the concept of morality does not itself imply or promote any particular moral perspective. When we say that moral reasons are ultimate reasons, we have still not said that they have to be particular kinds of reasons (such as an appeal to God's will, or to the interests of other people, or to the principle of love) or that only certain reasons can be called moral. If we said this, we would clearly be setting up one particular moral perspective as our standard to the exclusion of others, and we would be implying that if a person does not hold the "right" moral reasons according to our standard, he does not have any moral beliefs at all. We say, therefore, not that a moral reason has to be a particular kind of reason but that it must be, for the person who holds it, an ultimate reason—one which can override all other reasons or motives. Because of their ultimacy or overriding power, moral reasons can be said to constitute the governing principles of a person's life or the determinants of his lifestyle.[3]

People might well understand the concept of morality in this way and yet disagree about what is the right or wrong thing to do in a certain case. One person, for example, might think that ultimate importance should be given to the security of his family and of the society; in such an instance he might in fact be willing to sacrifice his own life or to take the lives of others in order to maintain that security. Another man, however, might believe that God's will ought to be followed and that taking the life of another human being even in time of war is contrary to God's will and ought never to be done. Clearly, these men would disagree, but even so, each would be giving moral reasons for his decision if he defended it as the ultimate reason for action. People may and certainly do disagree about what they consider ultimately the best action; our point is only that they are thinking and speaking morally when they defend the actions they advocate as the best, all things considered.

Of course, the reasons we give for our actions differ in important ways. Some of the opinions and beliefs that motivate people's actions are really nothing more than personal preferences: some people like football,

French food, and jazz; others prefer modern art, baseball, and classical music. However, some of our opinions are more important than these: we think that children ought to be taught to read and write, that all able people ought to pay their share of taxes, and that the law ought to protect private property. Some of the things we value hold such importance for us that we would be willing to take quite forceful measures to defend them—the right to vote, freedom of speech and religion, and equal employment opportunity. It is indeed characteristic of our normal decision-making that we consider some reasons more important than others.

In view of these differing degrees of importance some philosophers have spoken of hierarchies of moral principles or of a scale of priorities among values, but we should not conclude from this that in order to have a moral perspective one must be able to arrange his principles or values in a definite pattern or hierarchy. Although philosophers have noted the relative importance of different reasons or motives for acting, many have also been very suspicious of definite theoretical schemes. Whatever arrangement is suggested, people will always disagree over the specific ordering of priorities. Often when a person is especially puzzled about a moral decision, it is because he holds two principles which he values equally.[4] And many of our most difficult social problems are ones in which values actually recognized by people on both sides of an issue are in inconflict so that the question is one of relative importance. Absolute freedom of speech, for example, can endanger people's security if that freedom is used to incite riots, and it is not immediately clear in some cases (at least it has not been obviously clear to the Supreme Court of the United States) whether free speech or mildly endangered security is more important.

So, by saying that moral principles are characteristically ultimate or overriding considerations, we do not mean to imply that the whole of any single moral perspective can be reduced to a very few basic principles or that people often establish for themselves a definite or simple scale of priorities. The fact that people hold principles and that some of them can be discerned neither requires nor implies absolute consistency. Consistency is indeed an ideal because one must establish priorities in order to come to actual decisions. Priorities are determined in the same way that principles are originally established, but the moral perspectives and lifestyles that people hold are seldom absolutely finalized or consistent; indeed, a reasonable flexibility of moral principles may even be considered a mark of maturity.

It is interesting to note, in view of this characteristic of moral thought, that many social problems which have recently been raised as political issues are recognized and discussed as questions of "priorities." Exactly what is meant by this talk of priorities is not always clear, but we suggest that it is implicitly recognized in these discussions that the issues are fundamental questions of moral value or moral principle.

As far as moral education is concerned, we can lead students to recognize the priority of moral reasons over other reasons for actions and of the hierarchial character of moral values by "pushing" them to give the best reasons they possibly can for whatever decisions they make. Young people, of course, will normally produce reasons of personal preference or personal interest first. But a persistent Socratic questioning (and we imagine this being done in discussion with another student rather than by the moral education teacher) can move them beyond the personal interest stage to higher moral considerations.

On a more advanced level most decision situations involve more than one moral principle and are thus almost always open to the question of which is more important, for example, security or freedom of speech. Young people may even develop a sense of these alternative reasons for actions before they come to any clear understanding of what a moral value or principle is. Decision situations which do not yield a clear choice lead to a more thorough examination of the consequences of actions and to a greater sensitivity to the importance of moral considerations. So in discussing moral issues with young people it is usually possible to ask "Which is more important?" or to develop a comparison of the alternative reasons as well as the alternative choices: this leads to a question of priorities.

## NOTES

1. We use the terms "motive" and "reason" interchangeably here in an effort to keep our concept of morality as broad as possible. In answer to the question "Why did you do that?" either a motive or a reason might be given or, for that matter, an excuse ("he held a revolver to my head"). It will appear eventually that "reason" is the better term in this context because actions which people would

usually defend as moral choices are characteristically well-thought-out decisions. Certainly, "unconscious motives" would have to be excluded as the basis for moral decisions, but we also like to keep our concept somewhat broader than is often implied by the term "reason"; moral decisions can involve an appeal to emotions or feelings which might not be ordinarily thought of as "reasons," especially in a scientific age such as ours.

2. P. H. Nowell-Smith, *Ethics* (Baltimore, Md.: Penguin, 1954), pp. 307-8.

3. Speaking philosophically, we take this point to be analytic; nor do we consider this detrimental to our approach since it is a matter of the definition of moral. Whatever a person's ultimate reasons for action are, this simply *is* or constitutes his moral perspective.

4. It is this fact, often neglected by social scientists, that prevents moral decisions from being made by the kind of logical calculation done by computers or other technological devices. Without a definite and absolute priority scale it is difficult to program a computer even if all relevant information can be supplied.

# 5

# Philosophical Analysis II:
# Universals and Ideals

## THE UNIVERSALITY OF MORAL PRINCIPLES

Thus far in attempting to arrive at a common understanding of the nature of morality, we have said that moral decisions are matters of principle for those who make them and that moral reasons take priority over other reasons or motives for actions.

A third characteristic of moral thought comes to light when we consider the following situation: John has lent five dollars to Bill, but when he later tries to collect, Bill refuses to pay. In similar circumstances, however, Bill gets rather angry with Tom, and in an effort to get his money back insists that it is morally wrong for Tom to refuse to pay his debt. Tom, in turn, suggests that it is then equally morally wrong for Bill to refuse to repay John. Bill objects to this suggestion and insists that while it is morally wrong for Tom to refuse to pay, morality does not enter into the case of his, Bill's, refusal to repay John.

Obviously, Bill is trying to have it both ways, and his inconsistency shows something about the nature of moral thought. The situation would not be such an odd one had Bill not brought what he called moral considerations into it. He could have remained just plain selfish; the best way to be selfish (even the most consistent way) would have been to try to get his money back from Tom while at the same time refusing to pay John. But when Bill argues that Tom is doing something morally wrong in refusing to pay, he raises considerations of principle, and it is this that makes his inconsistency intolerable. Since he makes it a moral appeal, his statement implies the general principle that one ought to pay one's debts, and there is no reason why this principle should not apply as equally to his debt to John as to Tom's debt to him. In moral thought an individual is inconsistent if he refuses to apply the same principles to himself as to anyone else. Moral thought requires a consistency of this sort, so that if one refuses to apply principles consistently he is suspected of not thinking morally at all. If Bill continues to insist that Tom's refusal to pay is a moral issue but that his own refusal to pay is not, we suspect that he is just using the concept of morality for his own selfish purposes and is not taking it seriously at all.

This characteristic of universality is perhaps the most commonly recognized aspect of moral thought. It can be seen in the so-called Golden Rule, "Do unto others as you would have them do unto you" and in the common moral accusation, "How would you like someone to do that to you?" What this means is that when a decision is elevated to the status of a moral principle, it can no longer refer just to the particular individuals involved in the situation but must be taken to apply universally. Decisions which are considered matters of principle can no longer be stated as "I ought . . . " or "You ought . . . " but must take on a universal form, "One ought . . . " or "No one ought . . . " If it is morally right for me, then it must be right for anyone; if you have a duty, then I would also have a duty if I were in the same situation.

In addition to committing oneself to particular actions and recommending certain actions to others, therefore, to take up a moral point of view is to consider what it would be like if others or if everyone acted in the same way. Only if one is satisfied with an impartial application of his decision can he say that he commits himself to it as a matter of moral principle or of moral right or wrong.

Most people would easily agree that Bill is inconsistent and that he cannot really insist, on moral grounds, that others should repay him but that he need not repay someone else. The full extent and force of the universality of moral principles, however, is not always recognized. Unfortunately, it seems to be a part of human nature to try to claim more for oneself than one is willing to give to others. We "rationalize" our actions, as it is said, allowing ourselves to do things that we would not approve of others doing. People who pad an expense account, exaggerate their tax deductions, or "appropriate" company materials without a second thought are often outraged and indignant when they find others doing the same to them. And at times people treat others—those in lower paid jobs, public service workers, and members of minority groups—in ways they themselves certainly would not tolerate from someone else. "There but for the grace of God go I" is a pious reminder of the universality of our moral choices. This is not to say that any particular actions are in and of themselves morally wrong. It is only to say that morality requires consistency, so that when one decides and acts for moral reasons, as Immanuel Kant pointed out, he legislates for others as well.

One other aspect of the universal character of moral decisions can be illustrated by reference to the same example. If Bill were rather clever, he might still insist that he does indeed believe that Tom ought to repay him, that he need not repay John, and that he is not inconsistent in saying this. He might then explain that his universal moral principle is that people ought to repay their debts unless they are named "Bill" (and he might point out that this is why he personally always refuses to lend money to anyone named "Bill"). This clever move, however, would hardly let him off the hook, for one just has to insist that as far as the payment of debts is concerned, whether a person is named "Bill" or "Tom" is irrelevant. Principles apply in all essentially similar cases, and one cannot show that two debts are not similar merely by appealing to the names of the people involved. This might be emphasized by asking Bill—and this is also implied in the universality of moral principles—if he would recommend the same principle of repaying debts if his name were Tom.

Of course it is not always clear whether the factors appealed to by people in moral disagreements are relevant or not. Currently, for example, there is a whole flock of debated cases in which the issue is really the question of whether a person's sex is a relevant difference with respect to certain actions. Should divorce laws operate equally for men and for women? Or should men be allowed time off from their work when their wives have babies on the same basis that women are allowed such leaves? It cannot be too easily presumed that such cases are similar or dissimilar. The universalization requirement encourages us to compare situations and decisions, but it does not imply that every two cases in which only one factor is the same (telling a lie, for instance) must be judged in the same way. There are always many factors to be taken into account.

Since there is some inconsistency in the ways various philosophers use the terms "universal" and "general," it may help to clarify our understanding of their concepts. The term universal when used with reference to moral principles implies only that the person who proposes it is willing to apply it to all cases that properly fall under it regardless of his own or anyone else's involvement or noninvolvement, that is, irrespective of persons, unless personal characteristics make some relevant difference. It does not imply that the principle itself is a very general one in the sense of being intended to cover a wide range of cases. A universal principle can, in fact, be relatively narrow in its range. "Never lie to one's friend" is more restricted or less general than "Never tell a lie." Both, however, are universal. The claim that moral principles must be universal puts no requirements upon how narrow they may be. If, as philosophers say, there is no reference to particular people or objects, a statement is universal. The claim that moral principles must be universal is thus a much more limited claim than a claim that they must be statements of a certain degree of generality. To call a statement general (as opposed to its proper opposite, "specific") implies that it covers a broad range of cases. For our purposes we have left it open for moral principles to be as specific as one wishes. To call a statement universal, as opposed to particular, implies only that given the range it covers there can be no exceptions for individuals.

The universality of moral principles therefore should not be taken to imply that all moral problems can be solved by appeal to only a few basic universal principles. Situations differ in many ways, and many factors are relevant in each case. Since each of us must make many different and often unrelated decisions, we can be said to hold many different principles. In fact, the situations we face and the decisions we make are so varied and complex that it is not often that we actually think about the universality of our decisions at all. In most cases we hardly expect the situation to arise in exactly the same way again, so we only think about the factors at hand and satisfy ourselves that our decision is roughly consistent with our overall lifestyle or that it is in line with our own common sense.

It is probably true, nevertheless, that the moral principles we formulate consciously for ourselves are often rather general in the range of instance they cover. This has led some philosophers and moralists to insist that we should not rely upon general rules at all. Consciously trying to relate a complicated problem directly to a very general moral principle, they say, may lead one to underestimate or overlook important aspects of the situation. For this reason some philosophers and moralists (those referred to as situationists or existentialists in particular) insist that moral decisions are best made with primary attention to situational factors rather than to the maxims or principles one holds. Traditional morality, they say, has become legalistic and is not sufficiently open to what is new and different in our age. There is much truth in this assessment: outmoded legalistic thinking, as indicated in our introduction, is a contributing force to the loss of moral sensitivity in recent years.

But the existential or situational perspective is not at all inconsistent with the analysis offered here. We have said from the outset that moral principles may well be considered to be the products of a person's individual decisions rather than rules or laws laid down in advance to which decisions must conform. And we have insisted that, whether they accept the guidance and authority of religious or cultural traditions or not, people really must arrive at their own moral beliefs. The universal character of moral principles, of which we now speak, requires only a seriously intended consistency in one's decisions. So while situationists and existentialists may be contrasted with other moral philosophers in that they emphasize the complexity and immediacy of moral decisions, few would hold that it is morally responsible to be inconsistent in the sense described here or, like Bill in our example, to make exceptions for oneself. Giving primary consideration to situational factors is thus not at all incompatible with viewing one's decision as universally applicable. We have indeed left open the question of whether the principles one holds are very general (in which case one's moral stance would be characterized as a "rule" theory) or very specific (in which case, although one might consider some rather general maxims to be relevant to personal decisions, one's moral judgment would better be characterized as situational or as an "act" theory).

Nor is it implied by our discussion of this characteristic of moral thought that it is unacceptable ever to change one's mind or to revise one's decisions and principles. The new principle would only have to be held, once a person's mind is changed, as universally as was the former belief.

By implying principles of action, decisions actually set precedents for future choices. One can, however, decide to go against his own precedent for a good reason, such as a realization that a different value of higher priority ought actually to govern the case. One can also, of course, revise his priorities, but a person gives up thinking *morally* if for no reason at all he goes against a principle he has adopted.

The educational correlates of this characteristic are rather obvious and need hardly detain us at this point. In being willing to universalize one's decision, (a) one must be willing for others to act in the same way, and (b) one must be willing to apply the same principle to other situations which are essentially similar. In classroom discussions of moral issues it is always appropriate to ask how happy someone would be if others acted in the way he recommends. Imagining oneself "on the other end of the stick" (in what is perhaps the original moral sense of this phrase) is an important part of the mental process of making a moral decision. In addition to the direct question of whether one would be willing to make the same decision a second time in a similar situation, discussion would also move into the more complex problem of determining whether or not two given situations are the same in all respects. Students would thus be impelled to describe and evaluate the actual nature of a situation and the consequences of their actions.

## VALUES AND IDEALS

On the basis of what has been said above, we can now describe more definitely what constitutes a moral perspective. We have noted that man makes individual or case decisions which develop into principles prescribing certain courses of action in certain circumstances. Second (and still without saying anything about *why* men make these decisions), we have said that the reasons people give for their decisions are ultimate or overriding considerations: moral reasons or motives take priority as the reasons or motives one is willing to stand by. And third, we have said that consistency in the application of moral principles is essential to a genuinely moral perspective; that is, a moral perspective has to be universal, applying equally to all people.

What finally needs to be said to complete this picture is that in order really to be thinking morally, the various decisions and judgments a person makes need to be related *to each other* in at least a roughly coherent way to constitute what might be called a moral perspective. The phrase "moral perspective" may be a bit obscure or vague. In using it we are implying that moral principles are characteristically mental and, as such, are a part of the overall mental framework or structure by which a person understands himself and the reality about him. A moral perspective is, then, the pattern of thought formed from one's adapted moral principles.

We do not mean to insist that people have to formulate the mental beliefs and principles they hold into absolutely logical systems. Most morally sensitive people hold values or ideals which can, in certain instances conflict with one another, but this does not undermine the moral nature of their decisions. Unless, however, there is some tolerable coherence among the values a person holds, he cannot really be said to have a moral perspective at all. It is characteristic of moral thought, therefore, that the decisions people make and the principles they adopt are held together in at least a reasonably coherent framework. We can refer to this conceptual aspect of moral thought as its "value" or "ideal" characteristic and speak, therefore, of a person's *value frame* of reference or of his *moral ideals*. It might well be noted that a number of religious notions would serve equally well as designations of this general framework or perspective. Values and ideals are a normal part of faith orientations or creeds; perhaps the most common way of speaking about this aspect of moral thought is in terms of religious (or humanistic) faith.

While most moral philosophers might initially agree that moral judgments are normally based upon a person's ultimate values or ideals, they often understand and describe this characteristic of moral thought in rather different and sometimes incompatible ways. Professor R. M. Hare, for example, has emphasized the role of the human imagination in creating moral ideals. "To have a moral ideal," he writes, "is to think of some type of man as a pre-eminently good type of man, or, possibly, of some type of society as a pre-eminently good one."[1] But to say that moral ideals are conceptual or imaginative projections does not imply that they are unrelated to the various moral principles a person holds. An ideal is, in effect, the collection of a person's moral principles—a single model or picture built in a fairly coherent and consistent way out of the many principles he holds. One of Professor Hare's most interesting contributions to our understanding of moral ideals is his suggestion, in the following passage, that they are related to historical, religious, and cultural traditions and that the ultimate justification of a moral perspective lies not in any intellectual proof of the truth of one's judgments but in the actual lifestyle it embodies:

> The truth is that, if asked to justify as completely as possible any decision, we have to bring in both effects—to give content to the decision—and principles, and the effects in general of observing those principles, and so on, until we have satisfied our inquirer. Thus a complete justification of a decision would consist of a complete account of the principles which it observed, and the effects of observing those principles—for, of course, it is the effects (what obeying them in fact consists in) which give content to the principles too. Thus, if pressed to justify a decision completely, we have to give a complete specification of the way of life of which it is a part. This complete specification is impossible in practice to give; the nearest attempts are those given by the great religions, especially those which can point to historical persons who carried out the way of life in practice.[2]

In contrast to Professor Hare's emphasis on the imaginative element is the view that moral values are dependent ultimately upon human nature itself. Such a view is exemplified in the writings of G. J. Warnock, who argues that the ultimate basis of moral decision is the general condition of human life—what is often called the "human predicament." "The general object of moral evaluation," says Mr. Warnock, "must be to contribute in some respects, by way of the actions of rational beings, to the amelioration of the human predicament—that is, of the conditions in which *these* rational beings, humans, actually find themselves."[3] Other philosophers go further than Mr. Warnock in their analysis and classification of man's biological and social needs and formulate the values and principles that are derived from these. The general thesis of this position, however, is that the value framework which constitutes the conceptual element of moral thought may be derived more from an examination of man's actual needs as a human being than from an imaginative picture of what one thinks the world ought to be like.

Still other philosophers, however, tend to doubt that people are very consistent or coherent at all in their adoption of moral ideals. Professor Peter Strawson has pointed out the frequency with which even morally sensitive people change their ideals. "Such [ideal] pictures are various and may be in sharp opposition to each other; and one and the same individual may be captivated by different and sharply conflicting pictures at different times. At one time, it may seem to him that he should live—even that *a man* should live—in such-and-such a way; at another that the only truly satisfactory form of life is something totally different, incompatible with the first."[4] It is unlikely that people's ideals change quite so frequently; certainly they do not shift "from one hour to the next," as Professor Strawson also suggests. But the real issue, as far as we are concerned here, is not the frequency of change but the fact that people do think morally by reference to ideals. On this point even Professor Strawson does not disagree. He begins his essay on the subject with the simple statement that "men make for themselves pictures of ideal forms of life," and the ideals of which he speaks (asceticism, personal honor and magnanimity, devotion to duty, dominance and power) are certainly what we wish to refer to as values or moral ideals rather than specific moral principles for specific types of cases.

It might be obvious already, just from the mention of these three moral philosophers, that our fourth characteristic of moral thought is one which will have to take into account a wide variety of opinions. It may, nevertheless, be possible to establish this point if our designation is sufficiently neutral and general. We should say, therefore, that this overall orientation or perspective can be given many names—a value framework or moral ideal, as we have mentioned, a world view, a lifestyle, or a religious faith. It can even be thought of as an important part of what constitutes an individual's character or personality. This is why morality used to be spoken of (by the proverbial school master) as a matter of forming good habits. Telling lies and breaking promises build up a general tendency to act in these ways: one doesn't become a habitual liar or an untrustworthy neighbor except by an accumulation of lies or broken promises. When we talk about the development of moral principles, therefore, we are also talking about character formation. Those who naturally think about morality more in terms of character can be assured that this is implicit in our account of the concept; they are quite welcome to develop these ideas for their own use.

Since we do not wish to exclude any of these understandings, we cannot be too confining in our description. We shall consequently refer to it only generally, as a value orientation or a moral ideal and hope that this designation might prove mutually acceptable. We basically are referring to whatever way individual decisions and principles are coordinated into a fairly unified perspective.

In regard to the need for an overall moral perspective when making a moral decision, we might reply in two ways. First, this value orientation of moral thought may be understood only as the collection of a person's moral principles—the set of individual values or ideals implicit in his actual decisions. Clearly, if a person is to maintain consistency (the third characteristic) and to have some priority structure (the second characteristic) in his decisions, he cannot make very many decisions before his principles will have to be coordinated. Therefore, if priority and universality really are characteristic of moral thought, then taken together they require a coordination of principles, that is, a value structure of some sort.

Second, moral thought, like any other human ability, is developed only with growth over a period of time. Undoubtedly, with the making of a first few (usually tentative and revisable) decisions on a consciously moral basis, an individual cannot be said to have already developed a conceptual framework. Some recognizably moral decisions might therefore initially be made without this conceptual element. And people with rather well-developed moral perspectives may later even face situations which are entirely new to them and be forced to make decisions which are essentially unrelated to their previous ideals and values. This is the way we develop new values and revise former ideals; moral thought, like other types of thought, is always a constructive process of integrating the new with the established. At any rate we need not insist on this characteristic as a prerequisite of any single moral decision. We contend only that it is characteristic of developed moral perspectives to have a conceptual element which holds decisions and principles together; this we call a person's value framework or ideal.

In the light of this characteristic of moral thought some of our most common ways of speaking about people's moral beliefs and opinions make good sense. We often identify people with certain associations, parties, or ideological schools. We say, for example, that a person is a "socialist," a "liberal," a "communist," or a "Christian," and what we really mean by the nametag is that his values and hence his decisions form a cluster identifiable with the values of one of these general ideological groups. Social and political "isms" such as these identify people's moral perspectives as much as any way of speaking and are more generally understood than the common philosophical classifications of utilitarianism or naturalism.

This characteristic of moral thought can be brought into an even sharper focus when it is realized that people generally hold two related but distinct types of ideals. First, there is the image that one has of oneself and one's own life. Here we have what is often called a personal ideal including personal aims, objectives, or goals—some image of what sort of character one is or would like to be.[5] One can imagine oneself as healthy, wealthy, or wise, or as a doctor, lawyer, or Indian chief. And such an ideal might well be patterned after a real (historical) or fictional person; this is what is meant when an individual is referred to as a moral ideal or hero. A great deal of our moral thought, especially the developing moral values of youngsters, takes the form of identifying with some ideal person.

Second, there is the ideal that each of us has of the society in which he lives or would like to live. Our lives are not lived in isolation from other people, and since so much of our action depends upon what others are doing, we need an ideal of society or a social ideal as well as a personal one. We might imagine a society that is democratic, free, or "open" as the best society, or one which is ordered and governed by law, or both of these. Social ideals are, of course, to some extent established in the legal structures of nations: a constitution is, among other things, a basic outline of a social pattern established for the society it governs. At any rate the ideals people hold can often be roughly divided into the personal and the social, an ideal of the "good life" and an ideal of the "good society."

A little reflection on this distinction will convince the reader that personal and social ideals must be related to each other. Try to think, for example, of an action which does not affect other people as well as oneself. If one takes a certain type of life as his personal ideal, then his ideal society must be one with which that personal kind of life is at least compatible. Life, liberty, and the pursuit of happiness are personal ideals, but they can hardly be attained in an oppressive society. Social welfare (understood as an equal distribution of the world's goods) similarly might be an impractical social aim in a completely laissez-faire or individualistic economic system. Social ideals and personal ideals are necessarily interrelated.

Ideals, both social and personal, should, of course, have some relationship to reality. When people are accused of being "idealists" (an accusation often used to attempt to get people to forget about moral considerations), what is sometimes implied is that the ideals they hold are so unrelated to, or so much at odds with, the real world as to be impractical or useless. This can, of course, be true of both personal and social ideals. One can try to become an Indian chief, a witch doctor, or an alchemist—or, for that matter, a miller, a cooper, or a blacksmith—in contemporary Western society, but there will be great obstacles to overcome. In the realm of social ideals, one can attempt to live by a principle of cooperation rather than by one of competition, but one takes his chances at this as well. We certainly do not want to say that unrealistic ideals are immoral, but the further they are from reality the less chance there is of their being fulfilled and the more chance of frustration for the individual who holds and pursues them.

At a number of points in this discussion we have mentioned things which often make moral decision rather difficult. We have noted, for example, that, given our natural human inclinations, it is not always easy to act as one would have others act. We also have recognized the difficulty of conflicting principles: it is not always clear which of two moral principles ought to have priority in a certain case, and when the same person holds both principles, genuine moral perplexity follows. In speaking about moral ideals we run into another such area. People with well-developed moral sensitivities are often, in the common usage of the term, idealists. Their principles and values always seem to be slightly at odds with the realities of personal and social life. Perhaps there is an idealistic streak in all of us: we would like to be a little more friendly or creative than we have been, and we would like to see equality and justice prevail socially and to have international disputes settled by peaceful means. But real problems arise when we do not know whether to act in accordance with our own ideals or with prevailing social norms—whether to do what one believes is right or what society or one's employer expects. There are no easy solutions to real moral problems, but sensitivity to them is important. The distance between people's ideals and the realities of the world around them is well portrayed in current drama and literature, arts which hold an important place in moral thought on its imaginative or conceptual side.

What we have said about this last characteristic of moral thought is undoubtedly more vague and flexible than our description of the other characteristics. There are two reasons for this. First, the other characteristics are closely related to the logic of moral language and to the established uses of terms and concepts and can therefore be described more accurately. Our last characteristic, however, is not a logical or terminological point; it is an analysis of the way people think. It is what many philosophers would call a "phenomenological" analysis, a term that may easily be applied even to Professor Strawson's observations about "the realm of the ethical." Not only is there more diversity among actual thought patterns than in the common meanings of moral terms, but there also are additional differences in the ways people understand their own thought. At any rate since thought patterns are more difficult to describe than logical patterns, the analysis of this characteristic is necessarily more vague. Second, this is the area of moral thought in which there is perhaps the widest and most serious disagreement among people who hold different moral perspectives, and since our analysis must be broad enough to include all of them, there are rather narrow limits to what can be said in a neutral description. This may, however, have its advantages in that we must ask the reader to examine his own thought to discover what sort of conceptual framework he has—what ideals, values, models, heroes, and so on, he has.

Our fourth characteristic of moral thought must, therefore, be stated in only the most general terms: the decisions people make and the principles they adopt are interrelated with their other knowledge and beliefs in a conceptual framework of ideals and values. To preserve the neutrality of this general description we can admit that literally any kind of reason or motive for action may be built into a moral principle as long as it conforms to the first three characteristics. (Though from one person's moral perspective, which is determined by his ideals, the ideals that others hold may certainly be judged perverse or wrong.) It is initially only necessary that a person have *some* reason or motive for acting and that he find *some* cause for making a decision, so that he can be said to have some basis for an evaluative preference and therefore some value or values. As a person makes more decisions, the combination of the second characteristic of moral thought (that moral reasons take priority) and the third (that moral reasons be considered universal) serves to establish or require a conceptual framework of some sort. We suggest that this conceptual framework is normally established when, as Professor Strawson says, "Men make for themselves pictures of ideal forms of life," or, as Mr. Warnock suggests, when rational moral agents have an understanding of the necessities implicit in the human predicament.

Education in moral values and ideals will quite naturally be concerned with students' views of the nature of life and society. The moral influence of people in our society and historical figures who are themselves accepted as ideals (Martin Luther King, Jr., or Abraham Lincoln) should not be neglected, nor should utopian pictures of the good society (*Walden II* or *Plato's Republic*) be ignored. Social ideals are also important in that people in society must come to some consensus about what values or ideals should be incorporated into the civil laws. The law itself and the court cases in which it is interpreted provide a wealth of material for class discussion of personal and social ideals. The realm of values and ideals is probably the aspect of moral judgment which comes most quickly to mind when one speaks of moral education. It holds an important place in our approach, but it should also be apparent that this aspect of moral thought is only a *later or final consideration* after thinking about decisions and principles is developed step by step. It might also be evident that our view of education is one which encourages youngsters to develop and consider their own ideals. Moral education thus cannot be a matter of direct instruction in values and ideals. We shall have more to say later about the educational implications of the various characteristics of moral judgment. Before that, however, we must turn to the psychological approach.

## NOTES

1. R. M. Hare, *Freedom and Reason* (Oxford: Oxford University Press, 1963), p. 159.

2. R. M. Hare, *The Language of Morals* (Oxford: Oxford University Press, 1952), pp. 68-69.

3. G. J. Warnock, *The Object of Morality* (London: Methuen, 1971), p. 16.

4. I. T. Ramsey, *Christian Ethics and Contemporary Philosophy* (New York: Macmillan, 1966), p. 280.

5. Personal ideals are often said to generate "prudential" motives or reasons, and it is sometimes said that the term moral applies only to social actions as distinct from prudential acts. In the end, however, nothing is gained by restricting the term moral in this way since both the personal and social consequences of actions must be taken into account when real decisions are to be made.

# 6

# Psychological Analysis I: The Psychology of Moral Development

In this chapter and in the one that follows we shall deal with psychological approaches to the moral domain. The field of psychology, however, is divided into schools of thought or theory groups at such a basic level that we cannot attempt, as we did in the philosophical analysis, to find common agreement even on an approach to the moral domain. Not only are there differences of a theoretical nature in the field, but one often finds that psychologists who appear to be saying much the same thing use such different conceptual models and terminology that it is indeed risky to claim that they are in agreement.

## MORAL THOUGHT: A MICROPSYCHOLOGICAL ANALYSIS

In attempting to come to grips with this situation, we shall draw one rather general distinction which, artificial though it may be, can help to bring some measure of order out of the chaos. The distinction we have in mind is between psychological theories which are directed toward a specific analysis of the human mind and the way it works in moral decision-making, on the one hand, and theories of personal and social development, on the other. We take this distinction to indicate a difference in the level of analysis between theories concerned with specific thought processes and theories of a more general nature. Borrowing designations often used by sociologists to distinguish such levels of analysis, we shall refer to these theories respectively as micropsychology and macropsychology.

One benefit of this distinction is that we shall not feel bound to state exactly how micropsychological models are related to macropsychological theories. The distinction does imply that we are dealing with theories which are directed toward the same subject, but it also implies that these different theories approach the subject at such different levels that it is not possible, at present, to say exactly where they are consistent or inconsistent with one another. We do, in fact, believe that the cognitive development approach described in this chapter is quite compatible with the humanistic stance described in the subsequent chapter. We believe, furthermore, that it is instructive to attempt to discover the precise points of agreement and disagreement between these approaches, but we do not consider it very useful at present to attempt to combine these levels of analysis into a single picture. Our objective in this book is not a comparative study of psychological theories, and we cannot let ourselves be drawn into too much consideration of precise points of agreement or disagreement between psychologists. Artificial as it is, therefore, the distinctions that we have just drawn between the micropsychological interest in thought processes and the macropsychological analysis of human social development will have to serve to organize and coordinate our presentation. It may or may not be a distinction which helps to make sense out of the great diversity of opinion one finds in this field, but we hope that it at least clarifies our approach. We shall, accordingly, deal with psychological accounts of moral thought, the cognitive domain, in this chapter and leave other considerations of personal and social development, many of which are equally important for the task of moral education, for later.

## PSYCHOLOGICAL ACCOUNTS OF MORAL DEVELOPMENT

If only to acknowledge its formative influence before setting it to one side in view of our present purposes, we should first mention the classical psychoanalytic theory of moral development. From this perspective, based on the familiar Freudian model but perhaps best exemplified today in the writings of Erik Erikson, the child develops through a series of psychosocial stages related to his physical maturation. A psychology of moral development constructed on this analysis would have to pay close attention to the precise nature of the ego conflicts at each stage of human growth and would probably have to take into account the many personal and family factors which either facilitate or hinder the resolution of these conflicts.

While this kind of analysis could conceivably provide the psychological basis for a program of moral education, the difficulties of practical application seem insurmountable. The analytic approach requires a degree of sophisticated insight that cannot be expected of average school teachers, or even, for that matter, education specialists. Because of the complexity of psychoanalytic theory and the corresponding degree of expertise required, psychoanalysts have seldom recommended their model for use in the compass of a normal educational program. Education, to put it briefly, had best remain at the level of dealing primarily with man's conscious thought, rather than with his individual personality development or the unconscious factors that influence it.

The possibility of an important contribution to the field of moral education from this perspective, however, should not be too quickly ruled out. Erikson's analysis of ego conflict resolution at the various stages of development provides insights which may well be incorporated into some future program of human or personal development, particularly for younger children. Psychoanalytic theory would seem especially relevant for early education in the skills and abilities which ideally are prerequisite to moral education (the ability to empathize with others, to treat others as equals, to interact with authority figures, and so forth.) It is still doubtful, nevertheless, that the psychoanalytic model can be used in any direct way in this effort, and it is certainly, therefore, best for us not to speculate further.

A second approach to moral thought at the micropsychological level is that of social-learning theory and behavioral studies. Recent research on obedience to authority, the acquisition of conscience, altruism and sympathy, resistance to temptation and the like has produced an impressive collection of findings on human behavior in specific situations and on how such behavior is learned. According to this perspective moral behavior is learned in the same way as other behavior is learned—through positive and negative reinforcement. Punishment of socially disapproved actions builds in youngsters an anxiety which is commonly identified as moral feeling or conscience and which helps to build self-control. Exemplary of this approach are Professor J. Aronfreed's studies of resistance to temptation and the internalization of prescriptions in children.[1] He showed, among other things, that youngsters react differently when punishment is administered at the initial moment of the transgression of a prohibition as compared with punishment delayed and that self-punitive activity, when punishment is withheld, can reduce anxiety. Other studies have demonstrated significant differences in the effects of punishments given with stated reasons as compared with punishments administered without explanation.[2]

While the findings of these studies are undoubtedly significant in their own right, the question of how these results relate to one another, other than on the assumption that social learning is a process of association or conditioning, is another matter. The behavioral approach is unified on the level of a research technique, but at a more theoretical level we find only a collection of generalizations about the significance and importance of the findings. In some respects this approach seems to end where one might wish to begin. For example, it would be interesting to discover whether there are significant differences in the kinds of reasons given with punishments or not. Without further work in this area we are left to assume that if moral education is possible at all, it is only a process of conditioning. Accepting this assumption would then seem to entail viewing moral education as the inculcation of a predetermined pattern of socially accepted behavior, as in the case of behavior modification, for which the desired behavior is determined in advance, and we cannot accept this conclusion without denying our intent to avoid indoctrination.

However, this rejection of the social-learning approach for our present purpose is not intended to imply that we consider this whole school of thought hopelessly deterministic. Further research on how individuals develop systems of values in which different effects become rewards for them may well begin to bring this perspective and the humanistic perspective we shall adopt into closer contact with each other. Although the behavioral school has produced little in the way of an overall account of moral development which could serve as the basis for an approach to moral education, it should be noted that some research on specific issues does provide important insights which may be incorporated into the approach we suggest. We shall speak later, for example, of one educational strategy that centers on specific moral issues such as truth-telling and promise-keeping, to which many of the findings of this approach are quite relevant.

A third micropsychological approach to the study of moral thought is the so-called cognitive developmental or structural approach which we shall describe in some detail. The essence of the cognitive approach is the analysis of the structure of human thought patterns at various stages or levels of human development from early childhood to maturity. This stage development is held to be both a natural maturational process and subject to influence from environmental factors. Viewed from this perspective, moral development can be comprehended in a manner which is not only intuitively impressive and supported by considerable research but also appropriate for use as the theoretical base of an educational program.

Obviously, the theoretical perspectives of these three schools cannot be combined into a single model of moral thought—certainly not into one which would provide a workable psychological basis for an educational program. Not only are the theories and findings of each of these schools different, but there also is really little if any agreement among them on the source or the nature of the basic facts to which appeal might be made when a theory is being constructed. In short, the disagreement exists on such a basic level that we cannot expect to be able to coordinate the results.

Since common agreement cannot be found, therefore, a choice of some sort must be made before we can proceed. This is not, however, as difficult a problem as it might seem. When all is said and done, there is little reason for using either of the first two approaches as the basis of a moral education program. The psychoanalytic approach is a highly sophisticated model, and psychoanalysts do not generally advise its adoption by educators. The results of learning research, on the other hand, are at best not yet formulated into a comprehensive model adequate for educational purposes and at worst tend toward a doctrinaire approach we cannot accept. This leaves us with the cognitive development approach, the results of which are indeed, as we shall attempt to show presently, directly relevant to the goals and purposes of moral education.

In addition to this choice by elimination, however, there are a number of things that can be said at the outset in favor of the cognitive approach. In the first place, of the three theories just mentioned cognitive development is in many respects a mediating position. Although there is, indeed, a rather fundamental disagreement between cognitive developmentalists and learning theorists, future research and middle-range theories of each of these schools may prove not only acceptable to those who hold the opposite perspective but also quite relevant to their more general conclusions. The structuralist, as we see it, should certainly not want either to discredit or to underestimate the value of the results of behavioral research. Similarly, although the psychoanalytic model begins from its own sphere of evidence, recent discussion in this school is bringing its position closer to the developmental perspective. Many developmentalists have certainly acknowledged insights gained from psychoanalytic theorists. While we have proposed the adoption of only one of the major alternatives in psychology, therefore, we do not intend to exclude concern for, and profit from, the other approaches.

In the second place, the cognitive development approach is not only directly relevant to an educational program in the moral domain, but it is also a perspective which is already familiar to educators. Teaching in mathematics, for example, has been greatly influenced by the results of cognitive research on the formation of concepts in other fields. One finds notions of "readiness" for learning and a general effort to adapt learning materials to a child's "stage" or "level" of understanding. Current use of the cognitive development perspective thus provides a ready-made background against which we can discuss the psychology of moral development.

But finally, and in our opinion most important, there is the matter of the coordination of a psychological approach with the philosophical analysis presented in the previous chapter. In bringing together a philosophical account of the nature of morality and a psychological account of moral thinking, there would seem to be room for a good deal of disagreement, philosophers saying that moral judgment is one thing, psychologists that mature moral thought is another. Fortunately, this seems not to be the case. While there are some discernible differences in terminology, there is rather broad general agreement between the developmental approach and the philosophical analysis developed in our previous chapters. For both, moral thinking is basically a matter of principles to which an individual is personally (or autonomously) committed and which he would be prepared to apply universally. For our purposes we find no essential disagreement between philosophers and cognitive development psychologists on the definition of mature moral thought.

As we now turn to a psychological account of moral thought, therefore, we shall be describing stages of thought through which individuals develop toward the moral maturity which we have already described philosophically. Effective moral education rests not only on a concept of mature moral thought (or, as John Wilson puts it, on a concept of the morally educated person), but it also requires some understanding of the process by which this thought develops. In order to be able to lead young people toward mature moral thinking, therefore, the moral educator must be able, first, to make some judgment of the character of his students' current moral thought and, second, to have some idea of what other and more mature types of thought might lead them along the path of moral growth.

We are not yet, however, out of the woods: the cognitive school is itself not entirely unified. There is, indeed, a general agreement among Piaget's numerous followers that stages of moral development can be discerned and that Piaget himself was right in characterizing these stages as involving a progression from egocentrism, through a heteronomous-authoritarian stage, to a stage of autonomy and cooperation. However, beyond this general agreement one finds a number of different accounts. Various developmental psychologists have described the stages differently, and there is some dispute as to the order and the sequential nature of the stages. Therefore, since the area of common agreement among these psychologists would not be definite enough to give us a workable model, we have chosen the research we find the most conclusive and impressive—that of Professor Lawrence Kohlberg. His analysis presents a fairly detailed description of the stages of moral development—certainly more detailed than other accounts—and is thus more useful for our purposes at this point. We shall, however, also offer a critique of the Kohlberg model by reference to other theories and research findings which we hope will convince the reader that his theory is by no means the final word on the subject.

## STAGES OF THOUGHT: THE KOHLBERG MODEL OF MORAL DEVELOPMENT

Central to any understanding of the cognitive developmental analysis of moral thought is the notion of stages of thought. Cognitive analysis is based on the idea that human thought develops through a series of discernible stages as individuals mature. By a "stage" of thought, which might also be called a phase or mode, psychologists mean that an individual's thinking is *organized* or *patterned* in a certain way, hence the designation "cognitive structure." Actually, the notion of a stage used in this sense is not terribly different from the popular usage when it is said, for example, that a child is "going through" a certain "stage." What is often meant by this common usage is that the youngster understands the world in a certain way, that he thinks in a certain pattern or only about certain things, or that he sees things in a particular light.

With regard to the moral domain, a stage of thought should be distinguished both from the content of any particular moral question and from the specific conclusion that might be reached. A stage might initially be thought of as a point of reference (the demands of the parents, the approval of friends, or the requirements of the civil law) in consideration of any moral problem by which a decision for or against a certain course of action is reached. But more than as a point of reference, a stage, or level, of thought implies that the person's whole way of looking at a problem is colored or structured by this orientation. A stage might be characterized as a person's total perspective or his point of view or orientation and would thus refer to the manner in which his mind structures or organizes its knowledge itself. The concept itself will undoubtedly become clearer as we describe briefly each of all of the six stages of the Kohlberg model. Although we shall characterize the stages in our own way, we do intend this account to be faithful to Professor Kohlberg's description and will reserve interpretation as well as critical comments until later.

*Stages One and Two.* As we move from infancy to maturity, the initial stages of moral thought are more or less what one might intuitively expect. At stage one, which can be roughly described as an obedience and punishment perspective, actions are judged largely by reference to their physical consequences. This mode of thought is undoubtedly based upon innate responses of pleasure or pain and is therefore described by some psychologists as an egocentric stage (although this term will apply to stage two as well). While people who think at this level do recognize social norms and understand the labels "right" and "wrong" as used by others, they interpret these norms and labels almost entirely as references to the consequences of actions, that is, as rewards or punishments for themselves. The judgment of an authority is significant not because the authority represents a social order or moral ideal of any kind, but simply because he is more powerful. The parent and the policeman are not so much right as they are stronger and therefore able to enforce their will.

At stage two the egocentric attitude remains, but it becomes opportunistic as well. "Human relations," as Professor Kohlberg describes it, "are viewed in terms like those of the market place. Elements of fairness, of reciprocity, and of equal sharing are present, but they are always interpreted in a physical pragmatic way. Reciprocity is a matter of 'you scratch my back and I'll scratch yours,' not of loyalty, gratitude, or justice."[3] Other psychologists often speak of this stage as being characterized by expediency or exploitation of human relationships.[4] Again, as at any stage of moral development, the person may well respond to ideas of good and bad or right and wrong, but his response will indicate that he still interprets these concepts in terms of the consequences of actions understood in the physical sense of reward and punishment. He may bargain with his friends or with the authorities, but he basically will be out for what he can obtain for himself. An action is wrong, therefore, or a choice is bad because it is painful or will bring punishment or because someone able to bring pain or punishment *says* it is wrong. At both stages one and two, therefore, actions are judged by reference to physical consequences and the power of authorities; the difference at stage two, however, is that the person is willing to cooperate with others and even bargain with authority figures in an effort to obtain rewards or avoid the undesirable consequences.

*Stages and Levels.* The similarity just noted between stage one and two—that they are both reward and punishment oriented—is taken into account in the Kohlberg model in that they jointly comprise the first *level* of moral development. Basic similarities are also noted between stage three and four and between stages five and six. The six stages are thus divided into three levels which constitute not a separate set of categories but a simplification of the stage account on a more generalized level of analysis.

The *preconventional* level (stages one and two) is so named because individuals at this level do not yet respond to problems from a perspective of any consciousness of social norms. This level can easily be described as egocentric in that individuals experience little or no internal desire to belong to society or to maintain its conventions. Rather, they interpret moral norms or rules "in terms of either the physical or the hedonistic consequences of action (punishment, reward, exchange of favors), or in terms of the physical power of those who enunciate the rules and labels."[5]

With stages three and four we move into what Professor Kohlberg calls the *conventional level.* Conventionality refers to the willingness to conform to the demands of society for the purpose of maintaining or supporting the social order. The order of society, whether it is a legal order (stage four) or merely an order of acceptable behavior in a certain social group (stage three), is seen as good in its own right; the individual is willing to give up some of the personal satisfaction attractive at stages one and two in favor of maintaining his position in the social order and of maintaining the social order itself.

*Stages Three and Four.* At stage three a person is influenced primarily by the expectations of others and is willing to conform to the social norms when rewarded by social approval. Professor Kohlberg calls this the "good boy"—"nice girl" orientation, referring to the individual's desire to earn these designations of approval and his corresponding eagerness to fulfill the stereotypical image of proper behavior for members of his social class or group. Adults, it might be noted, think in this way when they refer to idealized social roles as, for example, parents or teachers and make decisions for themselves on the basis of their images of good parents or of what teachers should or should not do. Also at this stage actions are for the first time judged at least partly with respect to a person's intent or motives rather than merely by reference to the consequences. There may be no strong logical connection between consideration of motives and social approval, but it does seem that if conforming to an image of a good person is what determines whether an action is right or wrong, then it is the intent or desire of the actor that counts, and his failure to conform may be disregarded as simply a mistake. In any case the approval of others—and this includes both the concrete element of actual approval of one's peer group and the abstract notion of conformity to an ideal type—is a more important determinant of action than punishment, pain, or the fear of either. A general designation of this stage might thus be "conformity to person."

Stage four is similar to stage three in that notions of conformity and the maintenance of the social order dominate the pattern of thought. In this mode, however, it is conformity to rules, whether they be moral rules or the laws of the state rather than conformity to persons, that governs the person's point of view. Actions which violate social or moral rules or the civil law are considered wrong regardless of the consequences. The civil law or a definite code of moral standards is considered to be the basis of order in society, and social order is seen as being good for its own sake. It follows from this that respect for the authorities who uphold the law or for moral rules of the social order is important, but "authority," a notion which can be understood in many ways and incorporated into various modes of moral thought, is not exclusively characteristic of stage four. Professor Kohlberg speaks of this stage as the "law and order" perspective and points out that this tends to dominate public morality in many contemporary cultures. "Conformity to rule" would perhaps be a better general designation for stage four than "law and order," however, since one may conform to moral rules rather than civil law. The difference between this stage and stage three can be seen in the way official sanctions or dishonor (arrest and conviction, or ostracism) come to replace the social disapproval that would influence the stage-three person.

*The Postconventional Level: Stages Five and Six.* As we move to stage five we again enter a new level of moral thought. Stages five and six are distinguished from stages three and four as postconventional, or autonomous, modes of thought rather than conventional or conformist. At the autonomous level, beginning with stage five but including stage six as well, "There is a clear effort to define moral values and principles which have validity and application apart from the authority of the groups or persons holding these principles, and apart from the individual's own identification with these groups."[6]

Stage five is a mode of moral thought in which actions are determined by reference to individual rights or personal values, although the demands of society are not yet excluded. What is right and wrong is seen ultimately to be a matter of personal autonomous decision, but because of the diversity of opinions among people, a public consensus of some sort is necessary for the sake of social order. People may have different moral perspectives, but since they must live in community with one another, some public legal norms of behavior must be established. This is thus characterized as a social contract orientation in which (at least in American society) it is held that the civil law ought to serve the needs of the majority and ought to be constituted through democratic procedures. While this mode of thought may seem as law-centered or rule-centered as stage four, it adopts not the perspective of the law-maker, whose task it is to draw up the rules that will benefit the majority (rule utilitarianism) and that will be based upon individual rights, but rather that of the law-enforcer, who maintains the social order. "The result," as Professor Kohlberg puts it, "is an empha- sis upon the legal point of view, but with an emphasis upon the possibility of changing law in terms of rational considerations and social utility (rather than freezing it in terms of stage four 'law and order')."[7] Stage-five think- ing can, indeed, be characterized as "legalistic" in one sense of the term, but law is not treated as an abstract or transcendent rule which is morally right regardless of what men think about it. The law itself must always be judged in the light of people's values and interests, even though the neces- sity of public censensus or social contract ultimately leads to the opinion that once a law is constitutionally or democratically adopted, it must be obeyed. Stage five is thus closest to the theoretical perspective of demo- cratic constitutionalism (the official American tradition), despite the fact that stages three and four may currently be the dominant modes of Amer- ican thought. The crucial issue between the two is whether the law is thought to depend upon individual rights or values or not.

Stage six is similar to stage five in that both are "autonomous" in re- lating moral judgments to the principles or values that individuals adopt for themselves. At stage six, however, a person's principles or values are themselves seen as forming a consistent and at least relatively coherent moral point of view. While the value of social consensus is likely to be one element of this perspective, it no longer holds the dominant position it had in the stage-five mode. There is also at stage six an increasing tendency to understand moral principles in more abstract terms ("act only in ways that you could prescribe universally," or "do unto others . . .") rather than as specific moral rules ("thou shalt not . . ."). Stage-six thinking is thus most likely to involve appeals of universal principles of justice, equality, and the dignity of the individual. In cases of a clear conflict between the demands of the law, principles such as these would be held to override the requirements of the law. We can define stage six, therefore, as a mode in which moral decisions are made by reference to autonomous principles to which an individual is committed in that he would be willing to prescribe the actions universally. The reader will undoubtedly note a similarity be- tween the sixth stage of moral thought and our earlier philosophical account of mature moral reasoning. This provides an important point of contact between the psychological and the philosophical traditions which we are attempting to bring together. The similarity is a real one and should be noted, although we shall shortly attempt to show that it is not quite the similarity Professor Kohlberg seems to think it is.

## ELABORATION AND CONFIRMATION OF THE MODEL

A mere description of the stage model does not, of course, constitute proof of its validity or accuracy; confirmation through empirical research is necessary. The evidence Professor Kohlberg and his collaborators provide is indeed impressive, although to many, ourselves included, it falls well short of providing a conclusive demonstration. Leaving aside possible criticism for the moment, however, we can clarify a number of aspects of the theory by brief reference to some of this work.

First, there is considerable evidence to the effect that the stages of development are sequential, that is, that individuals develop through these stages toward moral maturity and that the sequence, although not the timing, of this development is invariant. This is demonstrated not only in studies of the development in the same subjects over a period of years[8] but also, by implication, in the success of Kohlberg's testing procedures. Almost without exception people understand clearly the kinds of reasons given at stages below their own and reject these reasons as being less important than the reasons offered at their own stage. The same subjects also find reasons at the next stage higher more attractive than their own, but they are increasingly unable to comprehend the reasons offered at correspondingly higher stages.[9] We would not, therefore, find an individual thinking at one stage who had not progressed through the previous stages.

The educational implications of this are most important. It implies that one cannot simply teach mature moral (postconventional level) thinking to youngsters who are not prepared for it by previous development through the various stages. Moral education must be directed toward bringing youngsters through the stages of cognitive development step by step. In fact, people generally move only very slowly through the stages, and most adults in our society never reach the postconventional level (stages five and six) at all; thus, moral education, to be realistic, must aim at facilitating rather slow transitions from stage two and stage three, and from stage three to stage four.

Second, research findings tend to support the notion that human development through the stages of moral thought is irreversible. Once a person has adopted a higher stage of reasoning, he may still offer lower-stage responses to questions, but he generally accepts only the higher reasons as determinative and will not lose the higher orientation he has once developed.[10] The implications of this finding are comforting to moral educators. Efforts to facilitate development may help to bring youngsters to higher stages of moral thought, but it is not likely that they will induce regression. Education can, however, serve to reinforce lower-stage thinking in youngsters and thus arrest moral development.

A third set of research findings especially relevant to education indicates that transition from one stage to the next is most likely to occur when a person is: (1) challenged with moral problems for which his stage of thinking provides no easy answers, and (2) presented with responses a stage higher than his own.[11] In short, people are attracted to higher-stage reasoning when it is presented to them. The educational significance of this point is obvious: development can be facilitated through contact with or exposure to higher-stage thought. Developing an effective program for this, however, is not as easy as this may seem to imply, since it cannot be assumed that students are especially influenced in their moral thought by what teachers say. The influence of other youngsters and of the school environment itself may be more important than anything teachers can actually say.[12]

A fourth area of research which is only marginally relevant to our purposes is the cross-cultural application of this model. Professor Kohlberg has consistently held, and a number of studies have tended to demonstrate, that the stages of development he has outlined are universal. Regional and possibly even local differences (ghetto areas) in moral development can be understood as fixations or arrests of thought at certain stages of development, but this does not imply, according to Kohlberg, that the sequential character of development is changed or that some people are incapable of higher-level reasoning. To date, studies on this model have been conducted in some twelve or thirteen cultural settings.[13]

Other aspects of the model have been elaborated, and research confirming the stage sequence in both experimental and real-life settings is indeed impressive.[14] Analysis of subjects involved in the well-known Milgram tests of obedience and authority, for example, showed that 75 percent of the stage-six thinkers refused to inflict pain on another person as compared with only 13 percent of the subjects at lower stages.[15]

## A CRITIQUE OF THE KOHLBERG THEORY

As we noted at the outset of this chapter, the psychology of moral thought is not a field in which we can adopt an approach by appeal to common consent. In proposing the use of Professor Kohlberg's analytical model, therefore, we have had to make a choice of one approach in preference to others. Our choice was based upon the conviction that the cognitive development approach is the most promising general theory in psychology at least for our purposes and upon the relative adequacy of the Kohlberg model as compared with existing alternatives, which are really neither very fully developed nor readily available.

There are, however, a number of difficulties with the Kohlberg model which qualify our acceptance and use of it: the research available falls well short of confirming the whole theory, important concepts are either ambiguous or unnecessarily confusing, and the evidence supporting alternative cognitive development models is not to be ignored. Furthermore, we must completely reject Professor Kohlberg's account of moral philosophy and of the relationship of philosophy to psychology. The final criticism, indeed, constitutes a major objection to Kohlberg and to any educational efforts which are based upon his views of moral philosophy; it might be noted that well over half of Professor Kohlberg's writings are on the philosophical rather than the psychological aspects of his theory.

Our reservations on this score would in fact prevent us from proposing the adoption of the Kohlberg model for educational use at all if we were unable to separate the psychological model from its author's moral perspective and, most importantly, if we were unable to construct what we consider to be a better philosophical base for moral education. Because of our rejection of Professor Kohlberg's philosophical position, however, and because he himself sees this as so inseparable an aspect of his psychological model—a view apparently not shared by all of the early collaborators on this work—we definitely must say that our own approach to moral education should not be very closely identified with his views. We have, indeed, advocated the use of his account of moral development as the most workable psychological base for our task, but we have advocated only its provisional or tentative adoption as the best current formulation within the cognitive development school. From our perspective, therefore, Professor Kohlberg's theory is a good and useful example of the cognitive development approach. We are convinced of the value of this general approach, evident in the rather wide areas of agreement among the followers of Jean Piaget, far more than of Professor Kohlberg's version of it.

At any rate these reservations about the Kohlberg model which we must now elaborate need to be kept in mind not so much because they require immediate changes in the analytical model itself, although we do believe that other formulations might well be able to avoid these difficulties or because they render the model untenable in an educational program, but because we need to keep our minds open to revision in the light of new findings and/or rejection in favor of a better alternative, should one appear. It would be of no benefit to the field of moral education at this stage of its development for any single psychological model to be adopted as official doctrine. We have, in fact, attempted to express our own view here rather firmly because we fear that progress in the field of moral education may be hampered, at least in the United States, by a too easy acceptance of this one theory.

## STAGE AND SEQUENCE PROBLEMS

Kohlberg and his associates have argued very forcefully that moral development is a matter of sequence of stages, and it must be admitted that their evidence for this sequential character is most impressive. As Professor Kohlberg has put it, "These different modes of thought form an *invariant sequence*, order, or seccession in individual development. While cultural factors may speed up, slow down, or stop development, they do not change its sequence." [16]

Comparing Kohlberg's studies with other research in the field, one does indeed find a very general agreement on the nature of the sequence of stages, and this agreement has been noted by many researchers in the field. [17] However, there is by far more agreement on what in Kohlberg's description constitutes the three "levels" of thought (preconventional, conventional, and postconventional) than on the more specific six stages. The argument, therefore, is roughly to the effect that development takes place from (1) egocentricity, through (2) heteronomy, to (3) autonomy. Beyond this, however, Kohlberg's own efforts to show a correlation between his analysis and other models is rather unconvincing. [18] For example, Kohlberg divides the level of conventional morality, which can also be called conformist or heteronomous, into two stages: conformity to persons (stage three) and conformity to rules (stage four). Norman Williams, however, drawing upon the Peck and Havighurst classification finds that his data suggests that these two stages seem to be alternatives rather than sequences on the road from expediency to autonomy. Williams's analytical model thus includes what he calls parallel as well as sequential stages. Furthermore, Professor Elizabeth Simpson has recently pointed out that although Kohlberg is rather forceful in his claims of irreversibility and invariance in the stage sequence, the research to which he appeals has only demonstrated this among stages two, three, and four.[19]

Especially in need of explanation is the question of the relationship between the stage an individual is developing *into* and the stage he is *leaving*. In his analysis of the distinction between heteronomous and autonomous thought, Piaget felt that there was no way in which one stage of thinking led into the next or prepared the individual for the next step. Professor Kohlberg's analysis seems for the most part consistent with this. On the other hand, he cites some evidence to the effect that when a person is presented with a problem for which his thought stage is inadequate, he is impelled to question or give up that mode. This seems intuitively quite probable, but there is a difficulty with the notion of a stage of thought being "inadequate" for certain types of problems. Kohlberg had originally spoken of a stage as something of a total world view into which all experience could be incorporated. That is, any specific experience could be interpreted by the individual according to his present mode. In particular Kohlberg has argued, against the associationist or learning-theorist approach, that changes in thought patterns are not dependent upon specific experiences because situations can be understood equally adequately on any stage. At this point it seems that he is indeed willing to say that there are situations to which a person's current mode of thought is inadequate and force him to develop a new thought pattern. A good deal obviously depends upon how this notion of "adequacy" is understood, but we have neither theory nor evidence that would add much to solving the problem. It does seem, however, that the more we learn about the transition from one stage of moral thought to another, the closer the cognitive development approach comes to an association model of social learning. The difficulty can be stated as a dilemma: either there are crucial moral issues for which thought at a given stage is inadequate, in which case the transition can be explained as a matter of social learning rather than cognitive development, or each stage is a total perspective adequate to all moral issues, in which case the presentation of crucial moral issues will not facilitate development because there are no issues to which a given stage is "inadequate." The nature of this field, we might add, is such that any one analytical model can ultimately be shown to be unsatisfactory only by comparison with one which proves to be more powerful. Given the nature of the available research, we suspect that it is possible to interpret the basic evidence (people's responses to cases or questions) to confirm almost any number of hypothetical models. Other models have in fact been suggested. In addition to Williams's refinement of the Peck and Havighurst schema just mentioned, Derek Wright has proposed a character typology which seems to combine cognitive stages of moral thought with certain kinds of character traits.[20] One might also mention Norman Bull's model which, although based upon a relatively weak analytical scheme, is nevertheless supported by a considerable collection of data.[21] Each of these approaches proves in its own way to be more complex than Kohlberg's pure intellectualism.

## GENERALITY AND SPECIFICITY

The next series of concerns stems from research as old as the Hartshorne and May studies published in the late 1920s.[22] These investigations strongly suggested that individuals think in different ways about specific moral issues rather than in any consistent pattern about moral questions in general. But if moral thought is thus situation-relative or situation-specific, either the notion of the stages must be given up altogether, or it must be allowed that the same individual might think at different stages with respect to different moral issues at the same time.

Norman Williams's research at the Farmington Trust Unit in England tended to show that moral thought was somewhat situation-specific, but he has also argued rather convincingly that a tendency toward generality of moral thought is one aspect of moral development, an important one of which moral educators might take note.[23] The latter idea correlates rather well with our philosophical analysis of the concept of morality, which seems to imply that prescriptivity precedes universalization.

In terms more compatible with Kohlberg's analysis it might be suggested that if moral thought is more specific than general, an individual may think at one stage for one issue or group of issues and at another stage for other problems. This is an open question—at least we are not now aware of any studies of generality and specificity on the Kohlberg model. However, the fact that dominant stages of people's thought can be determined according to Kohlberg's analytical model would seem to indicate that moral thought is fairly general. On the other hand, it might yet be discovered that some new kind of topical division of issues or situations will make the character of people's thought even more clearly determinable. Here we can only say that Kohlberg's theory, like all worthwhile theories, generates problems for future research.

## STAGES OF MORAL DEVELOPMENT

Another difficulty with Professor Kohlberg's model is its failure to clarify whether the stages of moral development are to be conceived as strictly consecutive, so that attaining a new mode of thought requires leaving behind the previous modes, or as cumulative, so that the attainment of a new stage involves a continuation and perhaps a reinterpretation of the previous modes of thought. Kohlberg's original view, following some indications in Piaget, was that the stages are consecutive to a point of being mutually exclusive, but this opinion was certainly more implied in his studies than actually demonstrated. Professor Elliot Turiel, to whose research the theory of cognitive development owes much, has done some work on this issue in which he argues that the transition from one stage to the next involves a restructuring and displacement of the preceding stage.[24] Since, however, the difference between restructuring and displacement is not at all clear, this sheds little light on the possible cumulative nature of moral development. Norman Williams, who has not documented his conclusions any more successfully than Professor Kohlberg and his collaborators have, holds an almost opposite view. The final stage of moral thought, according to Williams, "is one in which the individual has a number of different and simultaneously existing modes of moral thought which relate to a given situation." In addition to the indications drawn from his research Williams points to the evidence of everyday experience as follows:

> Most of us refrain from stealing from a shop. Naturally, since the reader is a sensitive and intelligent person, this is because he has worked out that the consequences are harmful to the shopkeeper, and if his example were followed, to society in general. But it is *also* because he would go to prison if he were caught: *and also* because authority is against it; *and also* because he would be ashamed of himself if his friends knew; *and also* because he feels it just wouldn't be right. And so on.[25]

Finally, although it is not directly relevant to our concerns, we shall mention Elizabeth Simpson's impressive criticism of Kohlberg's claim that this typology of stage development is universal.[26] She has shown not only that the evidence is rather weak and the research techniques questionable but also that abstract moral principles (justice, equality, the value of life, and so on) to which Kohlberg appeals are culturally biased. We shall attempt to demonstrate presently that these concepts are philosophically unsound when employed as Kohlberg uses them; she has shown that they are scientifically unacceptable.

Our major criticism of Professor Kohlberg's theory, however, arises from his efforts to identify his highest stage of moral thought with a particular philosophical concept of justice. His description of stage-six thought as embodying what he calls a general principle of justice is not clear at all. He claims that it is a formal definition (a description of the nature of moral thought rather than of a particular moral system) and that there is a fairly high degree of agreement among philosophers as to the formal properties of moral judgments.[27] Yet the philosophers who have tried to make sense of his account seem mostly to feel that it is based upon a substantive or normative principle (such as respect for persons) and is thus not purely formal as Kohlberg believes.[28]

The difficulty arises, in our opinion, because of Kohlberg's assumption that autonomous moral thought which he initially, and we believe rightly, identifies as the highest stage of cognitive development must always be based upon a principle of justice. Kohlberg's concept of justice, however, is itself unclear. In one article within the compass of a few pages he identifies it with (1) the preservation of the rights of individuals, (2) a universal mode of choosing, and (3) respect for persons.[29] The preservation of rights and respect for persons are actually not the same thing because the notion of individual rights carries many implications which the concept of a person does not necessarily hold, and vice versa. The real confusion, however, is that these two principles, each of which is a substantive and therefore not a formal principle, are equated with the formal notion of the universalization of a prescription. This confusing identification of two different kinds of concepts is objectionable because many principles other than individual rights and respect for persons can be universalized and can stand as the basis of stage-six thinking. In advancing this substantive philosophical opinion that all moral principles can be ultimately reduced to the principle of justice, not only does he make the absurd claim that the principle of justice has been and is held by men universally, but he also implies that Western philosophers (Kant, Mill, Hare, Ross, Rawls, and Dewey) are in agreement on this point. In drawing this conclusion, he does not attempt to define the concept clearly. Had he done so, he would have realized just how many different meanings the term justice can have. As Elizabeth Simpson has said, "Highly abstract concepts such as justice have so little commonality in meaning from one group to another as to be practically useless as cross-cultural generalizations."[30]

Kohlberg's confusion on this point has some rather obvious practical consequences. In fact, it leads him to exclude from stage-six thinking any mode of thought that does not appeal to respect for persons or the rights of individuals, regardless of how principled or autonomous it might otherwise be. This leads, in turn, to a tendency to characterize the stage-six thinker exclusively as one who is willing to put the rights or interests of individuals above the demands of the law in an act of civil disobedience. However, if civil disobedience is the only type of moral issue separating a stage-five thinker from a stage-six thinker, as it seems all too often to be in Kohlberg's writings, then his analysis is based upon a substantive principle (that respect for persons can override the civil law) rather than upon a cognitive structure (the principled character of thought itself). That this is true of Kohlberg's analysis can be seen in his examples of stage-six thought, all of which are cases of civil disobedience; he judges Socrates as a stage-five thinker because he obeyed the law (which he did not in fact always do), and he describes Dr. Martin Luther King, Jr., as a stage-six thinker because he broke the law. The analysis suffers from what Ludwig Wittgenstein called the fallacy of having only one example. In this case, however, the criticism is especially damaging because having only one example makes the distinction between stages five and six turn upon such substantive criteria of justice as respect for persons rather than on the formal criterion of universalizable or principled thought.

The question is whether Kohlberg has drawn an adequate distinction between stages five and six or not, that is, a distinction which is truly based on cognitive development rather than on differing moral opinions. It is at this point, therefore, that we have to cut short our adoption of Kohlberg's analysis. We accept his distinction between stage-five and stage-six thought as a difference between social contract thinking and principled thinking. At stage five it can be said, the individual recognizes that different people hold different values but insists that the value of social consensus (be it via civil law or not) overrides any and all other values that people hold. At stage six some of these other values are held to override, at least on occasion, the value of social consensus. We cannot accept the implication, however, that the stage six value par excellence is respect for persons or individual rights or the general principle of justice interpreted in this way. Our analysis in Chapters 4 and 5 led to the conclusion that in order to have a truly moral value an individual must be willing to universalize his judgment, but we did not go on to specify that judgment as one of respect for persons or individual rights. In fact there are many other moral principles which can be universalized and, therefore, held as a basis for decisions that meet the criteria of stage-six thinking. There are, indeed, many grounds for civil disobedience other than respect for persons, and Kohlberg is simply wrong in saying that rule utilitarianism (which we do not believe to be ultimately distinguishable from act utilitarianism anyway) would not justify civil disobedience.[31]

We therefore accept Professor Kohlberg's basic description of stage-six thinking as autonomous and principled, and we take this to be identical with the conclusion of our philosophical analysis. We do not, however, accept the additional conclusion that the principle of stage-six thinking must be one of justice as respect for persons or individual rights. Although respect for the rights or interests of individuals is an important moral principle, for the purposes of moral education the definition of morality should not be limited to exclude other possible moral principles and thereby many nonutilitarian perspectives.

This objection to Kohlberg's analysis is thus directed at an aspect of his theory which we have not presented as an integral part of his model of cognitive development. Since we consider Kohlberg quite wrong in adopting the philosophical position that all universal moral principles can be reduced to the concept of justice, we have deliberately attempted to formulate our own account of the pyschological model and our philosophical analysis of the concept of morality in a way which will avoid this criticism. The objection, however, is an important one; it is the focus of the differences between the approach we are proposing and the approach advocated by Professor Kohlberg.

## EDUCATIONAL USE OF THE STAGE ANALYSIS

The application of this kind of psychological model to classroom activity is a difficult task. The model itself is reasonably complicated and requires an ability to draw relatively fine distinctions. It is a tool which cannot be mastered overnight, and a teacher should not assume that he can apply it easily.

One reason it is a difficult analytical model to apply is that we are not ourselves accustomed to reflecting on the nature of our own moral thought. Many of us, it must be admitted, are relatively inexperienced in the moral domain—not in terms of decision-making, but in the sense that we have paid little attention to the structure of our moral decision-making.

Although application of the model may be difficult, however, moral education teachers should be able to develop the necessary insight and skills. Moral education is not a subject that can be taught without preparation. Even if the more puritanical forms of indoctrination are successfully avoided, moral education discussions can quickly degenerate into a series of useless bull sessions. The success of any moral education program depends, therefore, upon the development of skilled teachers. Certainly, no one could ever provide "teacher-proof" material, as it is sometimes called, which could merely be "administered" to students.

To return to the issue at hand: although various testing devices can be used to determine any individual's level or mode of moral thought, precise calculation of each student's level of moral thought is not necessary for a program of moral education any more than it is necessary in mathematics or literature. A determination of the general thought level of the classroom group will suffice. The teacher should probably deal with student's responses collectively and work toward a general analysis of class discussion rather than insist upon individual analysis.

Aside from the difficulties of precise individual testing, which Professor Kohlberg and his associates have noted more than once, the classroom is not a situation, at least as we envisage it, in which the teacher is normally attempting to influence students individually. Indeed, in a normal discussion class we have found that students influence one another to a great extent and that the teacher's input is largely a matter of stimulating the conversation; only occasionally will he challenge the general level of thought of his students by presenting an aspect of a stage or mode of thinking that is new to them. In the normal situation, therefore, the teacher will at most need to form a judgment about the level of thought in the group rather than about individuals.

Particular individuals will, of course, deviate from the general level of thought in the group, and special attention will surely have to be given to them. This, however, can be calculated after judgment has been made about the class as a whole as a question of deviation from the norm—an easier judgment to make than attempting to discern the precise level of each student's thought at a given time. We are suggesting, therefore, a group rather than an individual application of the Kohlberg analytical model. Individual testing may in some ideal sense be thought more desirable, but from an educational point of view it is both unnecessary and may have undesirable side effects (like IQ tests) of focusing attention too closely on precise stages of thought. Since the stages are not themselves rigid patterns, they should not and cannot properly be used for any rigid classification.

## NOTES

1. See J. Aronfreed, *Conduct and Conscience* (New York: Academic Press, 1968), and J. Aronfreed, "The Concept of Internalization," in *Handbook of Socialization Theory and Research*, ed., D. A. Goslin (Chicago: Rand McNally, 1969).

2. See A. Bandura and R. H. Walters, *Social Learning and Personality Development* (New York: Holt, Rinehart and Winston, 1963), and A. Bandura, "Social Learning of Moral Judgments," *Journal of Personality and Social Psychology* 11 (1969): 275-279.

3. L. Kohlberg, "From Is to Ought," in *Cognitive Development and Epistemology*, ed., T. Mischel (New York: Academic Press, 1971), p. 104.

4. See N. Williams and S. Williams, *The Moral Development of Children.* (London: Macmillan, 1970).

5. Kohlberg, "From Is to Ought," p. 164.

6. *Ibid.*

7. Kohlberg, "From Is to Ought," p. 165.

8. L. Kohlberg, "Stage and Sequence: The Cognitive Development Approach to Socialization," in *Handbook of Socialization Theory and Research*, ed., D. A. Goslin (Chicago: Rand McNally, 1969).

9. See E. Turiel, "An Experimental Test of the Sequentiality of Developmental Stages in the Child's Moral Judgments," *Journal of Personality and Social Psychology* 3 (1966): 611-618; and J. Rest, E. Turiel and L. Kohlberg, "Levels of Moral Development as a Determinant of Preference and Comprehension of Moral Judgments Made by Others," *Journal of Personality* 37 (1969): 225-52.

10. Turiel, "An Experimental Test of the Sequentiality of Developmental Stages in the Child's Moral Judgments," and E. Turiel, "Developmental Processes in the Child's Moral Thinking," in *Trends and Issues in Developmental Psychology*, ed., P. Mussen, J. Langer, and M. Covington (New York: Holt, Rinehart and Winston, 1969), pp. 93-131.

11. Rest, Turiel, and Kohlberg, "Levels of Moral Development as a Determinant

of Preference and Comprehension of Moral Judgments Made by Others," pp. 225-252.

12. L. Kohlberg, "Education for Justice: A Modern Statement of the Platonic View," in *Moral Education*, ed., N. F. Sizer and T. R. Sizer (Cambridge, Mass.: Harvard University Press, 1970).

13. L. Kohlberg, "Stages of Moral Development as a Basis for Moral Education, in *Moral Education*, ed., C. M. Beck, B. S. Crittenden, and E. V. Sullivan (Toronto: University of Toronto Press, 1971), pp. 23-92.

14. See N. Haan, M. B. Smith, and J. Block, "The Moral Reasoning of Young Adults," *Journal of Personality and Social Psychology* 10 (1968): 183-201 and J. Fishkin, K. Keniston, and C. MacKinnon, "Moral Reasoning and Political Ideology," *Journal of Personality and Social Psychology* 27 (1973): 109-119.

15. Kohlberg, "Stages of Moral Development as a Basis for Moral Education," pp. 78-79.

16. Kohlberg, "Stage and Sequence," p. 352 and Table 6, 3.

17. See Williams and Williams, *The Moral Development of Children;* D. Wright, *The Psychology of Moral Behavior* (Baltimore, Md.: Penguin, 1971); W. Kay, *Moral Development* (London: George Allen and Unwin, 1968); and N. J. Bull, *Moral Judgment From Childhood to Adolescence* (London: Routledge and Kegan Paul, 1969).

18. Kohlberg, "Stage and Sequence," p. 377.

19. E. L. Simpson, "Moral Development Research: A Case Study of Scientific Cultural Bias," *Human Development* 17 (1974): 81-106.

20. Wright, *The Psychology of Moral Behavior*, chap. 9.

21. Bull, *Moral Judgment From Childhood to Adolescence.*

22. H. Hartshorne, M. A. May, and J. B. Maller, *Studies in the Nature of Character*, 3 vols. (New York: Macmillan, 1928-32).

23. Williams and Willams, *The Moral Development of Children.*

24. Turiel, "An Experimental Test of the Sequentiality of Developmental Stages in the Child's Moral Development," pp. 611-18 and Turiel, "Developmental Processes in the Child's Moral Thinking," pp. 93-131.

25. Williams and Williams, *The Moral Development of Children*, p. 101.

26. Simpson, "Moral Development Research," pp. 81-106.

27. Kohlberg, "Stages of Moral Development as a Basis for Moral Education," p. 218.

28. See Also Professor Narveson's comments (B. S. Crittenden, "Discussion," in *Moral Education* ed., C. M. Beck, B. S. Crittenden and E. V. Sullivan [Toronto: University of Toronto Press, 1971]) and the essays by Alston (W. P. Alston, "Comments on Kohlberg's 'From Is to Ought', " in *Cognitive Development and Epistemology*, ed., T. Mischel [New York: Academic Press, 1971]), and R. S. Peters "Moral Developments: A Plea for Pluralism," in *Cognitive Development and Epistemology*, pp. 237-268.

29. Kohlberg, "Education for Justice: A Modern Statement of the Platonic View."

30. Simpson, "Moral Development Research," p. 96.

31. See R. T. Hall, *The Morality of Civil Disobedience* (New York: Harper and Row, 1971).

# 7

# Psychological Analysis II: The Humanistic Classroom

As we move from what we have called the micropsychological focus on cognitive processes to the macropsychological interest in total personality development and interaction, we are again confronted by a number of theoretical perspectives. Again we cannot allow ourselves to be drawn into the business of comparing and evaluating theories. There are, in fact, many perspectives which are quite relevant to our interest in the moral domain, and it would be unrealistic for us to attempt to sort these out. In any case we should not want to limit ourselves to the insights of any single theory. We shall, therefore, cite a number of theorists on the macropsychological level who have contributed to our understanding of the human personality and its development. We see no need to be exclusive, although in this chapter we shall be able to present only some of the insights which have influenced our view of human development and of the process of education. Our purpose is to establish an understanding of the environment or classroom atmosphere that is necessary for the facilitation of moral growth and to alert the moral education teacher to the necessity of being aware of this dimension. We would encourage those who are seriously interested in moral education not to neglect this area through overemphasis on philosophy or cognitive theory but to search out whatever insights seem relevant to their aims.

One approach to this dimension is based upon the distinction commonly drawn by educators between the cognitive and the affective domains. Since our last chapter dealt exclusively with cognitive processes, it might seem reasonable that we should now turn our attention to the affective domain. Indeed, most of the insights we shall mention here would easily fall within the scope of this domain. We do not, however, wish to emphasize the cognitive-affective dichotomy as it has been discussed in recent years, because we have found that it seems to imply too much of a division both of the person and of educational objectives. For this reason we have spoken instead of psychological analysis or theory at the micro and macro levels, a distinction which we take to imply a division of theoretical interest and research rather than a division of the person. In turning to all the many factors of personal development and interaction other than the cognitive process, however, we shall indeed be dealing with affective considerations.

## MORAL EDUCATION AND AFFECTIVE OBJECTIVES

Although the major contribution to the understanding of personal growth of which we shall speak in this chapter is drawn from the field of psychotherapy, we should first mention a theory of character development and an analysis of education which are closely related to theories of cognitive stages. The moral character study by Peck and Havighurst describes five stages of psychosocial maturation as follows:[1]

1. Amoral: Complete egocentricity, no internal controls on social behavior.
2. Expedient: "Conforms in order to avoid adult punishment or disapproval";[2] obedience to adults and compliance with rules are still egocentric, that is, for personal advantage.
3. Conforming: Accepts social and moral rules and therefore de-

velops a sense of right and wrong, but the rules are situation-specific, have no general meaning, and are not integrated into a coherent system.

4. Irrational-Conscientious: Rules become absolute and are internalized; conforming to rules becomes more important than social approval. (Stage four is an alternative to stage three.)

5. Rational-Altruistic: Concern for the welfare of others; flexible application of moral principles depending upon consequences for others.

Although the cognitive moral orientation of each of these stages is rather evident, Peck and Havighurst do not conceive these types exclusively as cognitive stages; they are not primarily describing structural changes in thought processes. They see them rather as total personality phases involving the individual's emotional (affective) orientation as well as his intellectual understanding. The Peck and Havighurst typology of stage development, however, does seem to lend itself to both cognitive and affective interpretations. On the one hand, Norman Williams's theory of moral stages mentioned in the last chapter is a cognitive reading of the Peck and Havighurst descriptions. The Krathwohl, Bloom, and Masia *Taxonomy of Educational Objectives*, on the other hand, includes an affective interpretation.[3] Both are valid understandings, but it is the latter in which we are now interested.

In establishing objectives for affective education, Krathwohl, Bloom, and Masia divide the domain into the general categories of (1) receiving, (2) responding, (3) valuing, and (4) the organization of values. (We shall omit consideration of the fifth category, which is concerned with the development of a total philosophy of life, because we find it indoctrinative. It is indeed a possible objective for educators since it is not outside the realm of possible education to see to it that students adopt a total philosophy or world view, but we consider this to be beyond the justified concerns of public education in an open and pluralistic society. There is indeed a strong suggestion in the *Taxonomy* that the authors have similar misgivings.[4] Teaching skills and abilities, even the ability to respond empathetically, is one thing, but adopting it as an objective so that students will internalize those abilities as normal aspects of their character violates the criterion of nonindoctrination we have established.)

The general nature of what is included in the *Taxonomy* under these

objectives is too well known to detain us long: receiving includes awareness, attention, appreciation, and so on; responding is described in terms
of willing compliance, acceptance or responsibility and enjoyment of self-
expression; valuing includes both preference and commitment; and the
organization of values requires both conceptualization and the formation
of a hierarchy or value system.

The authors of the *Taxonomy* validated their formulation by comparing it with existing research on moral development. They chose for this
comparison the Peck and Havighurst study, since, stemming from both
Freud and Piaget, this typology represents considerable thought and investigation. The happy conclusion of this comparison was that the taxonomy of affective objectives is consistent with this analysis of moral
development. We will hardly be going beyond the implications of this comparison, however, if we draw the further conclusion that moral education
must, at least in part, be affective education. The goals of moral reasoning
and decision-making require both cognitive and affective consideration.
As Krathwohl, Bloom, and Masia put it, "In fact, a large part of what we
call good teaching is the teacher's ability to attain affective objectives
through challenging the students' fixed beliefs and getting them to discuss
issues."[5]

The *Taxonomy* analysis and its correlate, the affective interpretation
of the Peck and Havighurst typology, enter into our proposal for moral
education in a most important way. First, it must be recognized that a great
portion of this domain is consistent with and in fact already covered by
what we have said about cognitive psychology since we have not interpreted cognitive processes as entirely separate from feelings. As we mentioned earlier, we cannot accept any strict division between the cognitive
and the affective, nor do the authors of the *Taxonomy* really propose such
a division. Our adoption of the Kohlberg model certainly did not exclude
the possibility of a more affective-oriented interpretation of the stage
development; we would certainly welcome such an expansion. It will be recalled that we left our adoption of the Kohlberg model open to such revision and reformulation by mentioning the Norman Williams and Peck-
Havighurst typologies as alternatives.

Even more striking, however, is the extent to which consideration of
the affective objectives has been included in our philosophical analysis.
The obvious agreement, we should hope, is between our account of the
fourth characteristic of moral judgment and the third and fourth general

categories of affective objectives—valuing and the organization of values into a coherent pattern. While we have avoided notions of systematization and have spoken rather of this patterning and coherence as the development of personal and social ideals, there is no essential conflict here; however, we still prefer our philosophical description because we consider the process not so much a rational one as an imaginative, visionary, or symbolic one. In fact, comparing our refusal to treat personal and social ideals as entirely rational constructions with the *Taxonomy*'s emphasis upon conceptualization and systematization,[6] our philosophical analysis seems almost less cognitive and more affective in its formulation than the descriptions offered by Krathwohl, Bloom, and Masia.

Recognizing the consistency with and coverage of much of the affective domain by our previous analyses, therefore, we should now bring this into full focus by stating more emphatically that the moral educator must indeed pay attention to the affective aspect or dimension of decision-making. Cognitive development cannot be separated from affective development. Young people, especially, often express their moral perspectives in terms of feelings rather than judgments, and they need to be aware of and appreciate empathetically the feelings of others in order to be able to foresee the consequences of their actions.

In general, however, it is our view that affective development (learning to appreciate others as well as to express oneself) is best fostered through the establishment of an educational atmosphere where "receiving," "responding," and "valuing" are encouraged, rather than by direct instruction. Rather than attempt to convert affective objectives (development through the affective hierarchy) into specific aims for moral education, therefore, our approach concentrates in theory on decision-making as an intellectual act and lets these considerations govern our view of the educational process in practice in the implementation of the program in the classroom. The humanistic classroom as we shall describe it later is one in which the teacher attempts to achieve a climate of personal trust, support, and empathethic understanding, a climate in which affective growth is fostered in unity with cognitive development.

Finally, we should note that the affective domain is not the exclusive preserve of the moral educator—nor, for that matter, is the cognitive. Accordingly, at the end of this chapter we shall have something to say about the relationship of the aims of moral education to the affective objectives adopted by educators in other fields.

### ROGER'S PERSON-CENTERED ANALYSIS OF GROWTH

One personality theorist whose perspective is especially relevant to education in the moral domain is Carl R. Rogers. In Rogers's view man can be pictured as an organism in the center of a field of experience. In this "phenomenological field," as he calls it, the self develops as a self-conscious understanding of the organism's focus. Man is thus an organism that has a center of consciousness in which symbols are used to form a structured impression of its own nature. The organism itself has basic needs and develops emotional responses; it exists in a real world and interacts with things and other organisms. The self is the organism's effort to comprehend its own needs, responses, and interactive exchanges in a coherent way. It may do this well, so that the self-concept accurately reflects the organism's states, or it may do a poor job of self-understanding if it misrepresents the world to itself or misapprehends its own needs and emotions. Human development is the process the organism in its self-conscious aspect uses to build, revise, and restructure this concept of itself. Development can be hampered or thwarted if needs, emotions, or the external reality are misrepresented, or it can move toward maturity as self-consciousness more closely approximates the actual state of the organism. Maturity, as the full development of a personality, is the point at which the conscious self attains an accurate picture of the total organism. In Rogers's words it is "a basic congruence between the phenomenal field of experience and the conceptual structure of the self."[7]

Brief and inadequate as this account may be, it might lead the reader to suspect that in Rogers's view moral development (he speaks more often of the adoption of values) is a matter of increasing self-awareness or, to use Abraham Maslow's term, self-actualization. It is the task of the psychotherapist to facilitate growth in self-awareness. The essence of Rogers's client-centered therapy is that the therapist provides the support and security which can help the client develop or restructure his self-awareness by replacing incongruous self-conceptions with more realistic ones. As Rogers puts it, "Under certain conditions, involving primarily complete absence of any threat to the self-structure, experiences which are inconsistent with it may be perceived, and examined, and the structure of self revised to assimilate and include such experiences."[8] The empathetic listening, as Rogers calls it, which characterizes the therapist's orientation toward his client directly facilitates personal and social adjustment, since through receiving empathetic support the client becomes more under-standing of others. Self-awareness thus leads to other-awareness. "When the individual perceives and accepts into one consistent and integrated system all his sensory and visceral experiences, then he is necessarily more understanding of others and is more accepting of others as separate indi-viduals."[9]

While education certainly is not a form of therapy, at least not a direct form, there are a number of respects in which Rogers's view of the client-therapist relationship has important educational implications. If teaching and learning is conceived of as, basically, an interpersonal rela-tionship, the qualities or attributes of the client-therapist relationship which lead to personal growth will also serve to facilitate learning. Rogers himself has described the qualities of a good teacher-student relationship under three headings.

First, there is what Rogers calls "realness." If human growth and ad-justment consist of increasing self-awareness, this will only be possible when reality (including the real needs and feelings of the organism) is not misrepresented. If the teacher-student relationship is a facade which hides both the teacher's and the student's real feelings, it will not facilitate real self- and other-awareness. By being open and honest with his students the teacher will help them to be open and honest about their thoughts and feelings with him and, in the process, with themselves and with one another. The best example a moral education teacher can give his students is his candor when formulating and expressing his own decisions. In con-trast to this, as Rogers sees it, is the classroom atmosphere in which the teacher is a walking textbook, without feelings or thoughts of his own, and the student is oriented toward trying to fulfill what he sees as the teacher's expectations by saying "the right things." Needless to say, this is not the sort of atmosphere in which the student can develop his own decision-making abilities, since moral decisions, by definition, must be based upon one's own thoughts and feelings.

The second characteristic of the client-therapist encounter which relates as well to the teacher-learner relationship is acceptance and trust, which Rogers calls "prizing the learner." What he has in mind here is the teacher's basic respect for the integrity of the student "as a separate per-son, having worth in his own right."[10] Only when a teacher respects the integrity of his students is he able to accept their thoughts and feelings, and only then will they share these with him. Students so often feel that a teacher knows so much more than they do that they are afraid even to ask a question, and teachers, some of whom are as insecure as their students, are often inclined to take student questioning as a challenge to their knowledge and authority. The way to break through this syndrome is for teachers to recognize that students usually do have important things to say. Students might not be experts on particular academic subjects, but they certainly can have valid intuitions. They can see relationships between the subjects they are studying and the real world.

The third characteristic is empathetic understanding, an attitude of attempting to see the world from the student's point of view. "This kind of attitude," writes Rogers, "is sharply different from the usual evaluative understanding, which follows the pattern of 'I understand what is wrong with you.'"[11] It is nonjudgmental and is as much a matter of feeling or intuition as of intellectual insight. However superficial or immature a student's concerns may seem at times, they are real enough to him and ought to be respected. With a little effort the teacher can enter into this world of concerns with all its symbols and emotions and can learn to appreciate the significance of events from the student's perspective. We should certainly not wish to make too much of the "gap" between the world of young people and the adult world; nor should we make too little of it. If empathy and appreciation are to be attained at all, the gap must be bridged *both* ways.

Taken together—and they are hardly separable—these attitudes form a relationship which is in many respects quite the opposite of the usual teacher-student relationship. When these relationships are developed between teachers and students in a group, one becomes aware of an entirely new classroom atmosphere. Students develop an honesty and openness which enables them to formulate and express their views and decisions more lucidly. The teacher correspondingly develops an ability to express his own opinions without putting coercive pressure upon his students to conform to his standards. The conclusion that Carl Rogers draws about this atmospheric change—that it constitutes something of an educational revolution—is not an exaggeration: "When a facilitator creates, even to a modest degree, a classroom climate characterized by all that he can achieve of realness, prizing and empathy; when he trusts the constructive tendency of the individual and the group; then he discovers that he has inaugurated an educational revolution. Learning of a different quality, proceeding at a different pace, with a greater degree of pervasiveness, occurs. Feelings—positive, negative, confused—become a part of the classroom experience. Learning becomes life, and a very vital life at that. The student is on his way, sometimes excitedly, sometimes reluctantly, to becoming a learning, changing, being."[12]

Bringing about such an educational atmosphere in the classroom is not easy. Most teachers have learned and internalized the orthodox professional role to such a degree that it is now difficult to break down the facade. Obviously we cannot prescribe a technique for being honest and open with students, although most of us who are teachers know when we are not. Some of the characteristics of the humanistic teacher, for example, empathetic understanding, can be translated into skills which the teacher can acquire and for which, if the basic attitude and desire are present, some techniques can be mentioned. We shall mention only a few and refer the reader to appropriate resources where they are available.

*Active Listening*. Especially when engaged in the discussion of moral issues, real feelings will be expressed or be implied just below the surface of what is said. These should be encouraged and used, rather than suppressed, in the classroom. One way for the teacher to keep communication of feelings open without overanalyzing or counseling is a technique described by Thomas Gordon in *Parent Effectiveness Training*.[13]

Active listening is the ability to feed back the feeling being expressed so that the speaker knows you understand what he feels. It does not imply acceptance or rejection of the statements the person is making, but it does communicate acceptance of the person and his feelings. When active listening is employed, feelings are communicated honestly because the communication itself is a process of negotiation: if the listener reflects a feeling somewhat different from that intended by the speaker, he is corrected almost immediately. If the listener does show that he has understood the feeling accurately, the speaker will not normally repeat it unless he wishes to express himself more accurately (feelings change in the process of expressing them) or on a deeper level.

Active listening has several benefits. First, the listener, in this case the teacher, does not get into areas of psychiatric counseling he cannot handle. He listens; he does not lead, guide, or direct. Second, both the dual monologue (both giving, neither receiving) and the inquisition are avoided; the door is left open for further communication. Through active listening the humanistic teacher feels respect for the worth and dignity of the student and, what is more important, he has a means of showing it. He shows that he understands and values students' individual thoughts and feelings by actively helping them express themselves.

*Education as Process.* The humanistic teacher must be able to recognize the signs that learning is taking place and know how to facilitate the process, especially how to keep quiet and let it happen. The kind of learning we are proposing does not always take place in neat, quiet rows. In fact, the best part of the process may occur when the casual observer would say that the teacher had lost control of the class. This is not to suggest disorder or chaos, however. In the discussion transcript in Chapter 9, the reader will find an example of an important interlude in a discussion which had been essentially (and not altogether needfully) teacher-centered up to that point. The teacher-facilitator was able to allow the group to carry on several discussions at once and then refocus the group. Most discussions of moral issues, furthermore, will end without closure. This is to be expected and encouraged. The teacher, then, must be able to tolerate incompleteness and refrain from summarizing, concluding, and wrapping up. The otherwise important teaching skills of concluding and summarizing are often best left unused if we expect students to be free to form their own decisions.

*Adaptability.* Since the humanistic teacher is more a facilitator of learning than an imparter of information, he must learn to accept and use feedback from the group. In doing this he will vary his approach to fit the situation, responding to students with enough freedom to adapt to their needs and desires and enough structure to keep the process on track. This is not always easy. We have found, however, that the more specific facilitating skills a teacher has acquired, the better he is able to adapt to the changing classroom situation. He will, therefore, need skills in structuring the physical environment and organizing activities such as role play, simulations and discussion skills. Discussion skills are especially important, of course, for the moral education teacher. One should not assume that no specific skills are required for running a good discussion or that it is only a matter of creating a disagreement or argument. There are many good books on discussion skills, including one by Stanford and Stanford which outlines a series of game procedures for developing these skills among students.[14] Discussion facilitation is an area in which all teachers need continual improvement.

The humanistic classroom, as we have so briefly described it, already exists for many teachers. Others agree with these goals but have trouble translating their goals into reality. We are absolutely convinced that no matter how good a program one may have, moral education cannot really take place outside of a humanistic classroom atmosphere. In many cases, therefore, if moral education is to be possible at all, changes will be necessary. It is clearly possible, however, for a teacher to change and grow—we know many who would like to—just as it is possible for a child. And help is available.

## MORAL EDUCATION AND RELATED FIELDS

Attention to the humanistic aspects of moral education leads quite naturally to consideration of other fields in which affective objectives are a central concern. Therefore, it seems appropriate to conclude this chapter with some brief comments on the relationship of moral education to other academic disciplines.

### *MORAL EDUCATION AND SOCIAL STUDIES*

A person whose intellectual development is at such a low level that he cannot foresee the consequences of even the most common human actions is unlikely to be able to make wise decisions. Teaching people to consider the possible consequences of various courses of action is, therefore, an important concern for the moral educator. The Schools Council Project on Moral Education in England has included this training as a regular part of its proposed program. "A practical concern with the consequences of actions," they say, "coupled with the disposition and ability to work out or visualize what may, or is likely to, happen next is essential if an individual is to treat others with consideration for their needs, interests and feelings."[15]

This should not be the concern of the moral educator exclusively, however. It is, or ought to be, one aim or goal of a general education in the social sciences as well. Teachers in related fields can adopt the specific objective of developing in their students the ability to foresee the consequences of actions in the light of all the relevant factors of concrete situations. A program in moral education might easily be seen as a continuation of what goes on in social studies courses and as a development of this on the level of personal decision and action. Coordination in this way not only can work to the benefit of moral education as such but also can contribute to the clarification of the aims of other social studies courses.

If such coordination cannot be achieved and the moral education teacher finds his students without the skill to foresee the consequences of their actions, he may have to begin there. It is perhaps more likely, however, that students will be able to think in this way but simply be unaccustomed to it; that is, they will be unaccustomed to visualizing the consequences of actions from different perspectives. In this case a program of moral education would have to begin by directing students' attention to this skill by giving them some concrete practice in predicting the probable or possible results of various actions. But while the ability to foresee the consequences of human actions is a prerequisite of good moral judgment, it is not necessarily a prior attainment or level of intellectual development. It is best viewed as a factor to which initial consideration must be given but which will be a continued focus of concern as moral education brings increased insight into human behavior. The whole area may be thought of simply as a matter of encouraging students to use their own common sense and imagination. People are not entirely wrong when they complain that youngsters today know a lot of facts but lack simple common sense. While this complaint is sometimes really a way of covering bigoted or prejudiced adult attitudes which youngsters rightly reject, moral education is indeed one part of the school curriculum where some specific attention can be given to the development of common sense.

## MORAL EDUCATION AND THE HUMANITIES

The necessity of having foresight into the consequences of actions draws attention to the way factual knowledge is relevant to moral decisions. Moral judgment is also, as we have emphasized in this chapter, closely related to the person's feelings, emotions, and attitudes. Educators are and always have been somewhat concerned with these aspects of the human personality: most of us can remember a teacher at one time or another telling us that he did not like our "attitude." The practice of giving students grades for proper or improper "attitudes" is still widely practiced.

As we consider education in the affective dimension of moral decision-making, however, we must again take account of our general aim and the criterion of nonindoctrination. In particular we have said that moral education which inculcates any single system of values or principles is indoctrinative and therefore unacceptable in an open society. However, if we now were to advocate the inculcation of certain attitudes, we would in effect be violating our own criterion; attitudes hold a position on the affective level similar to specific moral beliefs or principles on the cognitive level. Actually, we have serious reservations about the extent to which educators ought to influence young people in this area. Moral education, as we see it, should not aim at instilling proper attitudes any more than specific beliefs.

There is, however, one important aspect of this area which can be isolated and treated as a distinct ability (rather than an attitude). It is what is commonly called empathy. Empathy can be defined as the ability to understand others' feelings, emotions, needs, and interests—a general sensitivity to someone else's situation and to his point of view. While empathy is certainly an intuitive or innate ability in some people, it is also a talent which can be acquired or at least improved. It may be impossible to outline any series of steps for the development and exercise of empathy, but it seems equally true that with a little attention the talent can be cultivated. Most of us, teachers and students alike, would do well to pay renewed attention to its cultivation from time to time.

There can be little doubt that empathy is an important component of moral thought. One often feels that what is most needed and is perhaps most lacking in people's decisions and actions is a sufficient measure of sensitivity to the thoughts and feelings of others. This is especially important in a pluralistic society. Decisions of right and wrong in a given instance depend, to a large extent, upon the interests and feelings of those affected. Since cooperation is necessary for the fulfillment of one's ideal objectives, it does little good for an individual to develop his own values and ideals if in applying them he is utterly insensitive to the interests and feelings of others.

Recognizing the importance of empathy in moral judgment, therefore, we should say, as we did in considering foresight, that it may be necessary for the moral education teacher to attempt to develop this ability both prior to and along with the development of principles and values. Indeed, there may be times when the building of sensitivity to others is more important than some other aspects of moral thought. In moral education we continually need to be aware of the many dimensions of our objective and to be prepared to put aside for the moment what we might like to teach in favor of what needs attention. Surely the efforts of the teacher as facilitator in the learning environment will be directed at one time toward one aspect or element of the process and at another time toward another. It is an ideal, but certainly an impossible one, for the moral education teacher to be in control of all the many factors of the moral development atmosphere in the classroom at any one time. Realizing this, the teacher should rather pay his best attention to the obvious needs and periodically attempt to evaluate his efforts by criteria that can be drawn from consideration of each of the aspects of moral education separately.

In considering the element of empathy, the moral educator again, of course, recognizes the relationship of moral education to other disciplines. Sympathetic insight into situations and sensitivity to people's interests and emotions is an aim of the humanistic disciplines in general and of history, art, and literature in particular. If teachers in these disciplines are brought to see the relevance of their efforts to a program of moral education, they may well be interested in coordinating efforts, thereby relieving the moral education teacher of some of his responsibility for special attention to the empathy factor. Actually many teachers in these related disciplines already consider sympathetic insight into situations and sensitivity to others to be important parts of their educational goal. As an interdisciplinary domain moral education may well serve to relate the humanities to the social sciences in ways which can help to give our all-too-often fragmented educational curricula a new coherence and purpose. This happens, however, only as the moral educator recognizes the real importance and integrity of the many related disciplines, not when he attempts to make moral education a new subject in competition with established fields.

## MORAL EDUCATION AND THE COMMUNICATIONS ARTS

Even though a person may be sensitive to the needs and emotions of others, if he cannot interact successfully on a personal level with those around him, he may be unable to carry out his moral decisions through effective action. The development of social skills to a level of competence in interpersonal relations is another necessary factor in moral development. Moral education may thus have to be coordinated with a program of education in human relations. Much of what is necessary in this area is already, obviously, the focus of attention of education in the communications arts. The relationship between the moral educator's concern for decision-making and the communications teacher's concern for expression is reciprocal. The ability to express one's feelings and emotions accurately and effectively requires the clarification of one's point of view, which often includes one's moral perspective. Thought and expression exist in a reciprocal relationship; the more a person tries to express his thoughts and feelings, the more he actually develops and becomes aware of his own perspective.

At this point, however, we should like to enter a note of caution. There are a number of educational programs proposed and in use today which go well beyond communication into the areas of social relations and personal adjustment. Perhaps we are excessively conservative on this score, but we are inclined to think that great care needs to be taken in the use of such programs in the public schools. The techniques of facilitating interpersonal relations, techniques which were developed in sensitivity and encounter groups, are powerful tools which educators should adopt from their original settings only with utmost caution. We hope it will be evident, at any rate, that what we are proposing for moral education should not be confused with education in human social relations or personal adjustment. We mention this merely because we have discovered that many people, including educators, who do not see the moral domain as a distinct area of study, tend to confuse what we are proposing with recent proposals for education in human social relations or personal adjustment.

We conclude, then, that moral education presupposes and includes personal development in many directions. We have spoken especially of the development of foresight into the consequences of actions, of empathy and sensitivity, and of communications skills. Exactly what education is needed by any particular student or group of students at any particular time is a decision that must be made situationally. Moral education, as we see it, is certainly not a substitute for education in other areas; it is, rather, closely related to other fields in that it requires attention to the development of many skills and abilities. Nor should moral education be considered a cure for all the many problems young people face in modern society. It is only a part, though an important and much neglected part, of a comprehensive educational program in which all aspects of human development have their place.

## NOTES

1. R. F. Peck and R. J. Havighurst, *The Psychology of Character Development* (New York: Wiley, 1960).

2. Peck and Havighurst, *The Psychology of Character Development*, p. 98.

3. D. R. Krathwohl, B. S. Bloom and B. B. Masia, *Taxonomy of Educational Objectives: Handbook II: Affective Domain* (New York: David McKay, 1964).

4. Krathwohl, Bloom, and Masia, *Taxonomy of Educational Objectives*, pp. 165-66.

5. Krathwohl, Bloom, and Masia, *Taxonomy of Educational Objectives*, p. 55.

6. Krathwohl, Bloom, and Masia, *Taxonomy of Educational Objectives*, par. 4.1, 4.2, pp. 155-164.

7. C. R. Rogers, *Client-Centered Therapy: Its Current Practice, Implications, and Theory* (Boston, Mass.: Houghton Mifflin, 1951).

8. Rogers, *Client-Centered Therapy*, p. 517.

9. Rogers, *Client-Centered Therapy*, p. 520.

10. C. R. Rogers, *Freedom to Learn* (Columbus, Ohio: Charles E. Merrill, 1969), p. 109.

11. Rogers, *Freedom to Learn*, p. 111.

12. Rogers, *Freedom to Learn*, p. 115.

13. T. Gordon, *Parent Effectiveness Training* (New York: Peter H. Wyden, 1970).

14. B. Stanford and G. Stanford, *Learning Discussion Skills Through Games* (New York: Citation Press, 1969).

15. P. McPhail, J. R. Ungoed-Thomas and H. Chapman, *Moral Education in the Secondary School* (London: Longmans, 1972), p. 106.

# 8

# From Theory to Practice I:
# The Case Study Method

## EDUCATION AS AN ENVIRONMENT FOR GROWTH

In the preceding chapters we have described the three basic components of our approach to moral education. From an educational perspective we established our general objectives in terms of description of the
moral domain and its need for educational attention, and we attempted to
clarify the criteria of nonindoctrination by which education in this area
must be governed. Second, we presented a philosophical analysis of the
nature of moral judgment and, third, an account of the psychology of
moral development. Our task now is to draw these together into a more
definite plan for moral education and to describe the teaching methods we
consider most appropriate.

Looking at the domain from a philosophical perspective, we found
that moral judgments have certain characteristics by which they can be
distinguished from other reasons for action. They are decisions of prin-

ciple which hold the highest priority one is likely to give to any reasons for actions, are universal in nature, and are related to personal and social values and ideals. Moral education might be possible, we said, if people are brought to consider whether their decisions are good or poor in terms of these characteristics. These characteristics of moral thought can, we suggested, be formulated into questions or lines of inquiry by which decisions for action are brought into the light of a moral point of view.

An educational program to help young people develop this point of view must have two basic features. First, it must be centered on decisions about action and on stimulating students to raise the right kinds of questions about their own actions and about the decisions others make. Thus, it should begin with decisions concerning specific actions rather than with principles, values, or ideals since our understanding of moral thought implies that principles and values are characteristically built out of individual decisions that are not assumed or adopted prior to such experience. Moral thought, to put it one way, is inductive rather than deductive as far as principles and ideals are concerned. Therefore, in bringing students to consider their decisions from a moral point of view, that is, to test their thinking through the characteristically moral lines of inquiry, we will be helping them to build principles, values, and ideals in their own thought processes rather than giving them principles and values established by others. This is consistent with our criteria of nonindoctrination. We should thus begin with actual decisions about problems—moral cases as we shall call them—and try to influence students to think about them in certain ways rather than with ready-made principles or values.

The second feature of our plan for moral education is an emphasis on process or method rather than content. To think morally is to think in a certain way, to develop a moral perspective. Moral thought is not, therefore, a certain kind of, knowledge, for example, about the four characteristics of moral judgment or the six stages of moral development. To teach students this content amounts to teaching the analysis rather than the subject. The goal is not to teach students how to analyze the logic of human thought (philosophy) or how to discern different types of thinking (psychology). The purpose of moral education is to help students develop moral perspective for themselves. This purpose will be served only if we give students the opportunity to do some thinking for themselves so that they can develop moral perspectives of their own. The educational process will, therefore, have to be conceived as a matter of providing the kind of environment which will facilitate student thinking rather than one in which they are expected to learn some new content. Bringing these two features together, then, we can say that moral education from a philosophical perspective must (1) center upon particular moral decisions and (2) offer students the opportunity to do their own thinking.

From the psychological perspective the educational implications of the moral domain are remarkably similar to those drawn above. In considering the cognitive aspect of moral development we discovered that individuals normally progress through a series of levels or stages toward moral maturity. In this process of moral growth less mature thought patterns (the egocentric and heteronomous stages) are replaced by more mature ones (the heteronomous and the autonomous). Being thought patterns or cognitive structures rather than individual ideas, however, they cannot be directly learned or inculcated. Moral development is a process of growth through a wide range of experiences rather than a matter of direct learning or conditioning. Moral education, therefore, should be directed toward providing experience in decision-making within an environment in which normal growth toward moral maturity can take place and in which it can perhaps be facilitated. When this is provided, students are given the opportunity to test their thinking in practice and to discover the points at which their thinking is inadequate and/or is surpassed by better modes of thought.

From a psychological perspective, therefore, we are led to conclusions concerning moral education that are similar to those drawn from our philosophical analysis. The double focus described there is reinforced here: a program of moral education will have to (1) center upon particular moral decisions and (2) offer students the opportunity to do their own thinking. It is with this understanding of education as an environment for growth in mind that we suggest three teaching strategies: the case study method described in this chapter and the moral concept analysis and game techniques discussed in Chapter 9.

## THE CASE STUDY METHOD

Probably the most effective learning activity for moral education is the case study discussion. In this approach students are presented with a hypothetical situation in which an individual faces a decision; they are asked to consider the problem from his perspective and draw some conclusions about how they would act if they were faced with a similar decision.

The use of situation cases in education is not entirely new, but neither is it widely practiced. Were we to trace the history of this method, we would certainly have to mention the rabbinic tradition in Judaism and the teaching of casuistry in Christian moral theology. More recently, however, it has been used extensively at the Harvard Business School and by teachers of Christian ethics in American colleges and seminaries. Since 1967, case situations, or "critical incident materials" as they are called, have been a central part of the moral education materials developed by the Schools Council Project in England.[1]

The object of this activity is twofold. First, through considering the alternative courses of action, the consequences of one decision as compared with another, and the moral commitments that decisions imply, students can be brought through the experience of thinking out issues from a moral perspective. Each case study is thus a practice session for developing the skills and perspectives of moral reasoning.

Although the phrase "Socratic method" is often used (or rather misused) in reference to almost any kind of teaching technique, it is particularly appropriate as a description of the case study discussion. Socrates was known not for giving his followers answers, but for asking them questions, for posing problems in just the right way to aid their thinking. The present-day moral education teacher also can learn to pose the kinds of questions and thought tasks which will help students develop a moral perspective. In short, to think about decisions morally is to develop the habit of posing the right questions about the consequences of action, the principles implied in decisions, whether people should always do the same thing in a similar situation or not, what kind of society such actions would create, and so on. In focusing student discussion on certain issues, therefore, the moral education teacher bases his strategy on what we have described philosophically as the characteristics of moral judgment.

Second, the open discussion approach is also preferable to direct instruction for psychological reasons. Students will, of course, respond to the case problems with judgments and reasons that reflect their current stage of moral thought. During the discussion, however, they will face considerations which reveal the inadequacies of the less mature stages of moral thought, and they may discover that the kind of reasoning available at the higher stage is a more adequate moral perspective. One important objective of case study discussions is thus to attract students toward more and more mature thought patterns. This process, however, is a slow and developmental one rather than something that can easily be taught in a "lesson." Patterns of thought change slowly, and students are undoubtedly influenced more by their peers than by their elders and as much by everyday experiences (especially by the total atmosphere of the school) as by what goes on in class. The educator can provide an environment in which young people can have an opportunity to think out the various reasons for different courses of action in an experimental way, but he cannot control the great majority of experiences that influence students. There is some evidence, however, that such experience in moral thinking does help and that individuals who are presented with thought patterns slightly higher than their own are in a general way attracted toward more mature moral thought.[2] Our teaching strategy, therefore, must be to provide the environment for psychological development rather than to attempt directly to control or teach it. The case study method is clearly one of the better ways of doing this.

The case study method, therefore, serves two purposes: a philosophical one of giving experience in the skills of moral thinking and a psychological one of establishing a situation which facilitates normal moral development. Compatible as they are, however, these two objectives lead in somewhat different directions when one attempts to develop specific teaching strategies for them. If the philosophical objective is primary, one will be concerned to emphasize the development of students' thought processes and skills. If psychological development is the primary objective, one will be more concerned to encourage lively interaction which will challenge students and thus promote growth. Although these objectives are not at all incompatible, there is enough of a difference between them in terms of the teaching techniques appropriate to each to warrant separate teaching strategies. For the sake of organization we shall call the one appropriate to our philosophical objective the "rational" strategy and the one based on the psychological orientation the "conflict" strategy.

Although we shall direct the reader's attention to many important points of difference between these strategies, it is still perhaps best to consider them extremes on a spectrum of tactical approaches rather than mutually exclusive alternatives. This will permit the moral education teacher to imagine and develop a number of combinations or adaptations which will fall somewhere between these extremes. The best strategy for a class at any given time may thus be selected by the teacher from a whole range of possibilities between these extremes. For the present, however, we shall describe these extremes as genuine alternatives and emphasize the strong points of each.

## THE RATIONAL STRATEGY

At this end of the spectrum the objective is seen as the development of students' thought patterns in terms of some of the specific skills of decision-making: the ability to envisage alternative kinds of actions, the ability to assess the probable consequences of actions, and the ability to form some judgment of the personal and social values implicit in one's actions.

*Step One: Statement of the Case.* The first step is to present the class or discussion group with a hypothetical situation in which an individual is required to make some sort of action decision. It is best if the situation is open-ended or at least allows a number of alternatives—What should John do if he has been given responsibility for administering a quiz and he sees someone cheating?—rather than a case in which the alternatives are clearly limited—Should John report his classmate for cheating or not? The case may be presented in a written paragraph for students to read, or it may be dramatized in a role play or taken from a short story or film. Some of the best cases are simple ones drawn from everyday experience. Moral education as an integral part of a history or civics class, however, would use a series of materials drawn from law (legal cases are especially good) or from history. Here are two examples, one from everyday experience and one from history:

### 1. THE NEIGHBORHOOD STOREKEEPER

A group of young boys went into a neighborhood candy store every day after school. At first everything was all right, but soon they began to take things without paying for them. One day the owner caught them, and they admitted to him that they had been stealing candy for quite awhile. What should he do and why?

### 2. SOCRATES

Although he might be viewed as a professional philosopher now, Socrates was known in Athens as a local teacher and public figure. When he was about eighty years old, some of the people of the town were apparently offended by his criticism of Athenian life and by some of his teachings. A conspiracy developed against him, and he was charged before the court (which was kind of an emotional public forum of some five hundred "judges") with teaching atheism and generally misleading the youth of the city. He was found guilty and sentenced to death, though the judges may actually have wished to give him a lighter sentence. He could probably have obtained a punishment of being exiled from Athens; even after his sentencing it seemed that no one would have complained if he had been allowed to escape from jail and leave the city. His friends offered to arrange this, but Socrates refused to go. He said that he had been legally convicted under the laws of the city and that since he had always been a loyal citizen, he must continue to obey the law. He had refused before the court to stop his public teaching and must accept the court's decision. And so he was executed. Should he have done this, or what should he have done and why?

*Step Two: Finding the Alternatives.* The second step in a case discussion is to have the students search out the various alternative courses of action open to the subject. Although discovering what courses of action are open to the person in a situation may seem an obvious point, it is all too often neglected both in discussing hypothetical cases and in real life. We tend to see problem situations as either/or decisions rather than as situations in which some new, previously unconsidered course might be available. In teaching students to remain open to as many alternatives as possible, one appropriate line of inquiry is whether the options under consideration are really the only courses of action open to the person in the case situation, of if there are alternatives available. Jean-Paul Sartre, it might be recalled, thinks of moral decision primarily as a matter of discovering creative alternatives. Often in case discussions such creative alternatives appear as the pros and cons of decisions. In discussing the neighborhood storekeeper, for example, students often try later in the discussion process to produce a better alternative by combining aspects of earlier ones; for example, the storekeeper could tell the parents of the youngsters and also require them to work off the value of what they had taken.

Finding the alternatives can be accomplished in class discussion or as a task assigned to smaller discussion groups. Breaking the class into smaller groups has a number of advantages: it can allow for more individual participation by students, it is likely to produce a wider range of alternatives and consequences, and it demonstrates clearly to students that they are not simply being quizzed by the teacher for the "right" answer.

Although students will, of course, immediately want to form opinions about what they think the subject of the case should do, one important skill of moral decision-making that should be communicated (indirectly) is the willingness to postpone the decision until all the consequences and alternatives are considered. It is not especially detrimental if students take positions quickly, but as they gain experience in discussing moral issues, they will come to realize that it is better to find out all they can about a situation before committing themselves. This is an important skill of moral reasoning which can be communicated through the structure of the case study discussion and stands, incidentally, in marked contrast to the strategy at the opposite extreme of our spectrum.

Considering the case of the neighborhood storekeeper, students in a recent class came up with the following alternatives:

1. Tell their parents.
2. Call the police.
3. Ask them to work for what they had taken (without telling either their parents or the police).
4. Threaten to tell their parents if they do it again (in other words, give them a warning).
5. Spank them and send them home.

*Step Three: Calculating the Consequences.* This step is most important. As the first element of our philosophical analysis of moral judgment we said that moral thought is a matter of decisions and commitments which build into the principles upon which a lifestyle is based. A person begins to realize this, however, as he attempts to take account of the long-range implications of his decisions. We can, therefore, help young people develop a moral point of view by trying to get them to consider the full range of consequences of alternative courses of action and to understand those consequences by weighing the merits and disadvantages of each against the others. Our next line of inquiry after finding the alternatives, therefore, centers on judging the consequences: What is likely to happen? How are others likely to react?

In discussions of the storekeeper example the following consequences of the alternative actions are often mentioned:

1. Telling the youngsters' parents might not help the youngsters very much. Parents sometimes punish too severely (especially for

actions which embarrass them in the eyes of their neighbors); other parents defend their children regardless of the circumstances.

2. Calling the police seems too severe; the police might treat the matter too seriously.

3. Asking the youngsters to pay for what they had stolen by working for the storekeeper might not be effective. The youngsters might refuse or perhaps could not be trusted in the store anyway.

4. Threats can work sometimes, but if they do not, the storekeeper would have to do something else.

5. The storekeeper has no legal authority to spank neighborhood youngsters and might get into difficulty for this.

In thinking about moral issues, some people like to draw a distinction between the end, or objective, of a person's action and the act itself or the means to the end. They then point out that, as a matter of principle, the end cannot "justify" the means. This distinction is indeed comprehended in what we are saying about taking account of the consequences of actions. Considering all consequences includes whatever unintended consequences may result from the action itself (the means) as well as the consequences directly intended as the end or objective. In short as Professor Joseph Fletcher points out, the "end" includes the "means," because the consequences of the means cannot be separated or ignored in judging the full results of an action.[3] Thus, telling a lie (a questionable means) to obtain a cetain objective (a good end) results in the desired end and one lie, and this second consequence must be taken into account. The term consequences thus covers both ends and means, so that all is taken into account.

Since one can hardly trace the consequences of an action without forming some opinion of whether those consequences are desirable or undesirable, the third step in our case study outline is really continuous with the fourth step, in which students are asked to evaluate the reasons for and against each of the alternatives. In practice it is often most natural to let some of the pros and cons of each alternative be brought out as they are suggested. Our distinctions of finding the alternatives, tracing the consequences, and evaluating the reasons for and against each are primarily analytical or logical distinctions, steps in the logic of decision-making rather than necessary steps of programmed teaching. The way people actually think about decisions, however, does not and need not conform to this pattern. The analytical outline can be used simply as a checklist to see that all points are covered. We presume as the third step of a case discussion class, therefore, only that the teacher will in one way or another see to it that all of the alternatives and their consequences are considered. Much depends upon the particular teacher and his students. The style of the discussion can range from a very informal approach to a more organized "blackboard" outline of alternative decisions and their consequences. The class, as we mentioned, can be divided into small discussion groups, each of which would be given the specific task of listing the alternatives and tracing the consequences of each. Small group discussions should be specifically task-oriented, however, because a well-organized discussion can convey to students the fact that there really is some rationality to moral thought and that it is not all a matter of opinion or argument.

*Step Four: "Socratic" Inquiry.* The fourth step of the case discussion is testing the alternative decisions through a series of questions drawn from our philosophical analysis of the characteristics of moral judgment. This process of "Socratic" questioning will undoubtedly follow a random pattern according to the spirit of the discussion itself, and it is important to remember that we are still speaking of a class discussion process, not a matter of questioning or quizzing by the teacher. This process will be focused upon four general lines of inquiry.

a. *Separating Facts and Values.* One important point that emerged from our philosophical analysis of the nature of moral judgment was the separation of facts and values. Regardless of how facts and values are thought to be ultimately related, we said that it is helpful to the clarification of moral thought to attempt to separate matters of fact from matters of opinion or choice. A first line of questioning in case discussions, therefore, might be directed toward this distinction. Especially where there is a difference of opinion it will be helpful to attempt to reach a consensus on what the facts of the matter are. How can the facts be stated objectively? And what, on the other hand, is a matter of choice, opinion, or value? Where do the human choices really lie?

In the case of the storekeeper and the neighborhood youngsters the facts are rather clear; the real issue is faced when one inquires about the relative merits of each alternative decision. The facts could, however, be more obscure: for example, if one of the youngsters was a son of the store owner, there might be some doubt as to whether he was stealing. In most historical cases, such as the death of Socrates, there are definite questions of historical fact to be determined.

b. *Finding the "Best Reasons."* The second characteristic of moral judgment as we described it was that moral reasons or motives for actions take priority over other reasons and motives. We did not say why moral reasons are more important than other motives, for this is a substantive question on which we do not wish to take sides. Moral reasons are, however, characteristically the ultimate or final kinds of reasons a person gives for his decisions. Still, without attempting to answer the substantive question of why one reason is more important than another, we can direct class discussion of a case toward establishing the most important or best reason for a choice. If the cognitive development analysis of levels of moral thought is correct, this line of questioning should, over a period of time, lead students to accept reasons for actions at progressively higher stages. This does not happen all at once, of course, nor will students easily accept reasons which are above their normal stage of moral thought, but the search for better or more important reasons for actions should facilitate higher-stage thinking and, therefore, moral growth. Thus, we can direct one line of Socratic inquiry toward the discovery of better reasons and allow students to influence each other in the judgments they make with some assurance that their thought will develop in what most moral philosophers would consider the right direction.

The difference between attempting to facilitate moral growth and attempting to teach an advanced stage of moral judgment (as is often done in college ethics classes) will be apparent here. The moral education teacher will have to be prepared to deal with students on their own level and attempt to upgrade their thought through the interaction process. He will not be able to teach, for example, a stage five or six mode of thought to students who normally think at stage two or three. His objective will be moral growth and development rather than the attainment of a certain level of thought. What appear as the best reasons for actions to students may not be the reasons the teacher would consider best at all. He should accept this with the understanding that his task is to facilitate moral growth rather than teach any certain kind or level of moral judgment. Nor need he feel that he is condoning decisions or conduct of which he personally disapproves but which the majority of his students accepts. If the discussion environment is truly an open one, the teacher will be free to offer his opinion without its being taken as the "right" answer, and students will not feel that any decision, even one accepted by the majority, is ever being designated as the "right" thing to do in an absolute sense.

Asking students to look for the best reasons for choosing one alternative rather than any of the others available may also, if the discussion is a good one, lead to genuine conflicts of value, because the best reasons one can state for actions are those arising from one's most basic principles or values. Basic values can, of course, conflict with one another, so we are not implying that a thorough discussion of reasons for actions will necessarily lead to agreement. It is through this line of questioning that notions such as individual freedom, justice, and security can be seen to play a role in people's thought.

In class discussion of the storekeeper case, value considerations frequently come out as the basis of decisions. It is often said that because the storekeeper has to protect his store, he should call the police if necessary; another frequent comment is that the parents have a right to know about the incident and deal with it in their own way. In the case of Socrates the values involved are the importance of the law or of majority rule and the right to defend one's life.

c. *Considering Decisions as Universal Principles.* In describing the third characteristic of moral judgment, that moral principles are universal, we mentioned a number of ways in which specific decisions can be tested. Good moral judgments, we said, share a "Golden Rule" characteristic of being applicable to all people in similar situations.

In class discussion, therefore, one important line of "Socratic" inquiry will be to consider the situation from the perspective of each of the individuals involved. If one student states that the storekeeper should call the police, for example, we might ask if he would approve of that alternative if he were a parent. If it is said that he should consider asking the youngsters to work off their debt, we might ask whether this is fair from the youngsters' perspective or not. This does not imply, of course, that the best action in any situation is the one everyone approves; the youngsters would probably not be terribly happy with any of the alternatives open to the storekeeper. The point is rather that were the storekeeper in the youngsters' position, or the parents', or the police's, he would still have to be willing to accept the consequences of the decision he is proposing. In the discussion class this means that any decision in a case needs to be considered from the perspectives of all the participants.

Second, to test the universality of a decision the teacher should inquire about the possibility of applying it in essentially similar situations. In case discussions this can be done by considering similar cases or by altering the circumstances slightly to see how this would affect one's decision. Thus, with the storekeeper one would consider whether the incident happened in a small neighborhood community or in a large city and how this difference would affect one's decision. Would it matter if the storekeeper knew the parents of the children well, or if he knew the police and could judge how they would react? What if the stolen goods were more valuable than just candy? There are really a good number of possible modifications to each case, and considering them can help one decide whether he would be happy or unhappy with the same decision in all essentially similar cases. In each instance in order to be satisfied with one's decision and defend it as a universal judgment, one would either have to accept the same decision in a similar situation or show that the situations differed in important respects.

d. *Ideals and Values.* Finally, we come to what we described as the ideal aspect of moral thought: people's decisions and actions imply different views of what men ought to be and of the nature of society. For any decision, therefore, it is appropriate to ask whether the action in question is consistent with the individual's ideal picture of himself and with the kind of society in which he would like to live or not. This issue develops quite naturally from any discussion of values that might be raised by the previous questions, but it also has a more imaginative aspect. This line of inquiry might, in fact, be one of the most important aspects of moral thought for many students, since it can raise considerations which are recognizable as relevant to decisions on nearly every stage of moral development.

In our sample case one might consider the difference between a storekeeper who was willing to take the time required to deal with the youngsters personally in whatever way he thought best (speaking to the parents or having the youngsters work in the store) and a storekeeper who was only interested in running his business and would therefore deal with the situation as quickly as possible. One could then inquire generally about the differences between a society in which people settled problems personally and one in which they resorted to police or other official agencies. How legalistic should society be? Could we get along without certain laws? It will soon be discovered that in any class there are students who hold rather different images of the ideal society. Some are conservative in the sense of valuing security and the established structures of social life; others are more liberal in the sense of valuing freedom and social change.

These different ideals should, of course, be brought out and compared with due respect for the integrity of each. Our objective is to bring students to a realization of the nature and place of such ideals in individuals' lives rather than to promote any single perspective.

*Step Five: Making a Decision.* The final step of the case discussion is also the final step in moral reasoning, that is, making a judgment. Despite the length of the moral-reasoning process and the precautions against making a quick judgment, the decision itself is the most significant step. It is important, of course, that people actually learn to make decisions as well as to weigh the reasons for and against various alternatives. It is perhaps especially important for them to realize that most likely with difficult situations any decision will have at least some undesirable consequences. Learning to accept the consequences of one's decisions requires courage, but it is an important aspect of moral development. There comes a time when a person must make the best decision he can and then be willing to stand by his action.

Moral education, as we have emphasized all along, is not a matter of communicating a specific moral system. Students will naturally appeal to different reasons for their final judgments about any case. The class discussion will not necessarily move toward a consensus, and certainly the teacher should not coerce the class into producing the "right" answer or agreeing with him. The teacher will also undoubtedly have his own opinion, and it would be less than honest and open of him not to state it. He may, of course, wish to delay stating his views until students have come to their own decisions, but we have found that when the classroom atmosphere is properly developed, the teacher can indeed take a position without allowing his view to dominate the discussion. If there is a second teacher as a discussion observer, it may be helpful for the observer to enter his comments on the final judgment as well. This will give students a chance to see that adults do not always agree. The teacher can, in fact, indicate by his comments the ways in which his opinion was changed or influenced by the discussion itself, thereby affirming his own role as participant.

The actual method of asking students to make their own judgments will vary according to the nature of the class. In general, however, it may be best to ask them to write their decisions. This will give them time to sort out their considerations and come to a single conclusion. At certain times and with certain groups the privacy of stating one's own view without risk of being embarrassed or bullied into conformity is also important. Some determination should be made of whether individual students will be pressed into conformity or not before students are asked to commit themselves too strongly in public. An atmosphere in which differences of opinion and judgment are respected can indeed be developed, but it is a mistake to presume that it exists.

In summary, our version of the case study discussion might be outlined as follows:

1. Statement of the Case
2. Finding the Alternatives
3. Calculating the Consequences
4. Socratic Inquiry
   a) Separating Facts and Values
   b) Finding the "Best" Reasons
   c) Considering Decisions as Universal Principles
   d) Ideals and Values
5. Making a Decision

## THE CONFLICT STRATEGY

We shall now be able to describe the second case study strategy, the opposite extreme on the spectrum, by reference to its differences from the rational strategy just outlined. This approach has been developed in the Harvard University/Carnegie-Mellon University Moral Education Curriculum Development Project and is fully explained in their publications to which we would refer the reader. (The formulators of this strategy are not responsible for the name we have given it.)

In contrast to the emphasis on thought processes and skills which characterized the rational strategy, the conflict strategy centers upon the creation of a disagreement among students which will challenge them to defend their moral opinions or, hopefully, to develop better (that is, higher stage) ones. It is in the midst of such a creative conflict, according to the Kohlberg theory, that students find their own stage of moral thought somewhat less than adequate and are attracted to a higher one. This strategy can be formulated in four steps.

*Step One: Confronting a Moral Dilemma.* The differences between this strategy and the previous approach are evident even in the first step of the teaching plan. According to the conflict strategy, when a case is presented, it should pose only *one* clear option for students to consider: Should the storekeeper call the police or not? Or, should Socrates escape or accept the death penalty? There is no place in this strategy for the second step of the rational strategy outline, that is, finding as many alternatives as possible. The intent of the conflict strategy is to allow only one choice so as to create a difference of opinion.

*Step Two: Stating a position on the original or alternative dilemmas.* This intent is, furthermore, carried into the second step of this approach which is also specifically designed to heighten differences of opinion ("an effort to promote disagreement"[4]) or to create such differences if they do not already exist. In one discription of this approach this step is characterized as follows:

> Step 2: Stating a position on the original or alternative
> dilemmas
>
> In this step, the teacher ascertains the division within the class about what the major protagonist in the dilemma ought to do. Each dilemma ends with a question such as the one which follows: Should Fritz let the prisoners escape? In order to teach for cognitive moral development, the members of the class must divide over the answer to this question. If at least a third of the students in the class elect each position, the teachers moves immediately to Step 3, skipping the alternative dilemmas.
>
> If at least a third of the members of the class do not line up on each side of the issue, the teacher introduces an alternative dilemma from the lesson plan to establish a division among students. One set of alternative dilemmas has been designed in case the class agrees that the protagonist SHOULD take a particular course of action. Another set should be used if the class agrees that the protagonist SHOULD NOT take a particular course of action.[5]

*Step Three: Testing the reasoning for a position on the dilemma.* From this point forward the case discussion takes on the atmosphere of a debate either with students attempting to convince one another to change their opinions or with groups of students who hold the same opinion attempting to agree upon the best reasons for their position or the best criticisms of the other view. In step three of this strategy it is accordingly recommended that students meet in small groups consisting either of students who agree about the appropriate action or of students who disagree. This step is finally completed with a full class discussion in which decisions are tested through a series of probing questions designed to elicit what students consider the best reasons for one decision or the other and where they feel obligations lie. This step is not significantly different from the Socratic inquiry outlined in the rational strategy above, and we need not restate the lines of inquiry already elaborated. The probe questions suggested in the Harvard/Carnegie-Mellon materials are not, however, organized along these lines, although there is no reason why they could not follow this pattern, except that the approach of this project does not have the explicit philosophical base which served as our principle of organization.

*Step Four: Reflecting on the reasoning.* The final step of the conflict strategy is a process of summation and reevaluation. It is certainly not expected that the conflict will be resolved in any mutual agreement any more than it was supposed in the rational strategy that a consensus would be found. Students on each side of the dilemma should, however, have gained some appreciation of their opponents' views and should, therefore, be less dogmatic in their own opinions.

## STRATEGIES: PRO AND CON

Although it will be an important question for teachers, we need not spend much time here comparing these strategies. That each has its merits and its difficulties will be quite evident to anyone who experiments with them. The strong points of one strategy seem to be the weak points of the other, but since we have envisaged these approaches as alternate extremes on a spectrum, this leaves the moral education teacher free, as far as we are concerned, to find a happy medium or, better yet, to move from one extreme (perhaps beginning with the conflict strategy) toward the other (the rational strategy) as the needs, interests, and abilities of his students change. We shall limit our comments, therefore, to a brief mention of what we consider to be the shortcomings of each strategy as seen from the opposite perspective.

The rational strategy may prove to be far too analytical to keep students' interest and to challenge them sufficiently. Rational analysis is not a normal part of most students' moral thought; youngsters are likely to be impatient with efforts to trace out the details of a problem, and when they become impatient or lose interest, they may not be sufficiently challenged to reevaluate their own thinking seriously. Although the psychological evidence is not terribly refined on this point, it seems quite likely that students change their moral perspectives as much for emotional (affective) as for rational (cognitive) reasons. A moral education class in which the challenge provided by the conflict strategy is absent, therefore, may not bring students to an encounter at the most advantageous level.

The conflict approach, on the other hand, can fail to give an adequate impression of the rational process of decision-making. The strategy of raising a dilemma and asking students to take positions immediately can give the impression that making moral judgments is mostly a matter of taking and defending one's own initial, perhaps even unconsidered or purely emotional, opinion. It thus leaves out entirely the idea that decision-making is a rational process and promotes in its place the popular misconception that decisions are things that people argue about rather than reason through. Far from helping people in society work out differences or come to sympathetic understandings of other positions, this approach may even contribute to the difficulty many people in our society have of even discussing moral issues.

The conflict strategy can seem entirely adequate, however, only when the philosophical aspect of moral judgment is ignored. Philosophers do not normally recommend adopting moral positions first and defending them later; they usually suggest that all possible consideration should be given to an issue prior to making a decision. Following the rational strategy, students would be encouraged to avoid jumping to conclusions. Rather, they would be asked to consider the various possible courses of action open to the people involved, the consequences of each alternative, and the values implicit in them. Only later would the question of a decision be posed.

Both of these criticisms are, we believe, serious and deserving of consideration by moral education teachers. Strategy decisions, however, cannot be made without reference to the nature of the class involved and the teacher's particular abilities. At least initially we should think that the best strategy in terms of the likelihood of success in the classroom would be the one with which the teacher is most comfortable. One might suspect that student interest and involvement could be created initially by adopting the conflict strategy and the class might later move from this end of the spectrum toward the rational approach as students develop patience to consider all the contingencies of an issue and skill in raising questions for themselves. The development of these discussion skills should not, of course, be mistaken for moral (stage) development. As a general rule, however, strategy questions must be worked out situationally.

## HOT AND COLD CASES

Finally, we should mention one other aspect of the case study method on which the moral education teacher will have to make his own decision. This is the question of whether to deal with issues which are of current public concern and on which, therefore, students are likely to have strong preformed opinions or to choose cases which are equally problematic but more remote from students' immediate concern.

One thing to be said in favor of dealing with controversial issues, hot cases as they might be called, is that they easily arouse interest and thus lead to a lively interaction. They are especially appropriate, therefore, if one is working with the conflict strategy; a good division of opinion is easier to obtain if the issue is one students have considered prior to class. The cases which follow will serve as examples of hot issues; the first was written by Professor Barry Beyer, a co-director of the Harvard/Carnegie-Mellon project mentioned earlier.

### *AMNESTY DILEMMA*

As a representative to the United States House of Representatives, you are faced with voting for or against an important bill dealing with amnesty. The bill under discussion in the House calls for a general amnesty for all resisters and deserters. The bill specifically grants amnesty for all those individuals who refused to register for the draft and fled to Canada and other countries. It also grants amnesty to those in the military who deserted. Further, the bill ends immediately sentences for those convicted of draft evasion or desertion. In the House of Representatives, all attempts to amend or modify the bill have failed and the House has agreed on a roll call vote on the bill. As a representative you must now make a decision concerning your vote on the general amnesty bill.[6]

### *PRESIDENTIAL PARDON*

As a result of the Congressional investigation following the Watergate incident. President Nixon felt compelled to resign from office. The special prosecuter appointed for the case has collected evidence and is prepared to charge the ex-president with obstruction of justice. The trial would undoubtedly be a long one, but it is very unlikely that the former president would be acquitted. Before the case is brought to court, however, Mr. Nixon applies to the new President for an executive pardon for his involvement on the grounds that he was acting only in accord with what he saw to be necessary for national security and therefore in the best interests of the country. Assume that you are convinced of his sincerity and that in other cases this would indeed be reason enough to grant a pardon. If you were President Ford what would you do?

## *ABORTION LAW*

A bill has been introduced into the state legislature which would make any form of abortion illegal. As a representative to the legislature you will have to vote for or against this bill. Assume that you are generally opposed to the practice of abortion and would therefore be inclined to vote for the bill. A large majority of voters in your district, however, are opposed to the bill and have asked you to vote against it because, they say, you should not impose your moral views on others by law. How would you vote?

Although cases such as these can create a rather lively class discussion, there is also much to be said in favor of avoiding especially controversial issues. First, when students' minds are already made up, they may not be open to consideration of alternative actions. Rather than looking seriously at the alternatives and attempting to trace the consequences, they are inclined to discuss all sorts of irrelevancies. Avoiding hot issues may thus be best when one is following the rational strategy and wants students to think out the alternatives and their consequences before jumping to conclusions. In general the more controversial the issue, the less likely it is that the teacher will be able to direct students' attention to the intellectual process of decision-making. From a philosophical perspective, at least, the quality of moral thought is not always indicated by the heat of the debate.

Second, there is the practical consideration, which is quite important in certain school situations, that controversial issues may arouse public criticism or parental reaction. While we do not think teachers should always avoid subjects that are controversial, neither should we wish to see a moral education program needlessly attacked by those who do not understand its objectives. If public reaction is likely, as it is in many places today, one can devise relatively "safe" case materials by drawing upon historical incidents or court cases. The United States Supreme Court records are full of cases; since dissenting opinions are also published, several sides of issues are presented. When judges themselves are in disagreement, the critic of a moral education program would not be as likely to object to a teacher who refuses to tell the class which side of an issue is "really" right.

"Cold" cases, as they might be called, need not, however, be so distant from everyday experience that they do not engage the student's interest. All that is necessary is that they be issues which are not currently up for public debate. If a student has never considered a question before, he is more likely to approach it with an open mind, and when minds are open, there is a correspondingly greater probability of a class discussion actually working through the process of moral reasoning. The following are examples of "cold" cases which we have found to be at least as engaging as many controversial issues.

## VOLUNTARY EUTHANASIA

Imagine that you are about forty years old, the father of two teenage youngsters, and the sole supporter of your family. After a series of medical tests the doctor has recently told you that you have a cancer which has progressed too far for successful treatment. If you remain in the hospital, it is possible that you could live for six or eight months, but if you refuse hospital care, it is likely that you will die within three months. The hospital expenses, however, will far exceed the limits of your health insurance, and the balance, estimated at around $25,000, would have to be paid by your family. This would so exhaust their resources that it would not then be possible for your children to continue their education beyond high school, as they had planned, and your wife would be left without any form of property or security. You could, of course, absolutely refuse medical treatment that requires hospitalization. This would hasten your death, but it would also leave your family in much greater security after you are gone. What would you do?

### BROKEN WINDOWS

After a basketball game at your school a near-riot developed in the parking lot during which some windows of an out-of-town school bus were broken. The school principal and the basketball coach have apologized to authorities at the other school, but they have not been able to discover who was actually responsible for the damage. They have therefore decided to punish the whole student body by refusing to allow your local school busses to transport students to out-of-town games unless they discover who did the damage. At a meeting of the student council, of which you are a member, one student says that he saw the incident and is willing to tell the principal who was responsible if the council votes that he should. He also says, however, that he feels the situation in the parking lot was out of control and that everyone there was equally responsible so that it might be more fair for the whole student body to accept the punishment. How would you vote?

These cases are, of course, directed toward the interests of secondary school students. They may not, therefore, seem very problematic to adults, but it is important in moral education to deal with subjects which the students themselves see as moral issues. *Cases must be scaled to the moral level and interests of these who are being asked to make the decisions, or they will have little effect upon them.* Once an effort at moral education is underway, however, it is not uncommon for students to suggest case problems themselves. In one eighth-grade class students came up with the following role play: A man selling fruit from a stand on the street is passed by a policeman who says hello, picks up an apple, and walks off to the street corner. A moment later the vendor catches two boys taking apples and takes them to the policeman who is still eating the apple he took.

Discussion of such a scene would center on what each of the participants—the vendor, the policeman, and the boys—might say. Some students, at a higher stage of moral development, saw the incident as a case of injustice; others, at a lower stage, saw no problem since they assumed that the policeman (a symbol either of strength or of authority) could take what he wanted.

At this point it will be obvious to the reader that we have said little about the possibility of moral stage analysis of case discussions. Ideally, the teacher would be able to judge the general stage or level or his (or her) students' moral thought. In practice, however, this is quite difficult, and we should be careful not to categorize students too quickly. With a good deal of experience it may be possible for a teacher to form some opinion of the moral level which seems to dominate a class discussion and offer reasons for decisions at a slightly higher stage. Our experience, however, is that this is only occasionally possible, and we feel that such judgments are likely to be inaccurate. In any case this is not a necessary part of the teacher's task since it is just as likely to take place naturally if he raises appropriate questions. And according to Professor Kohlberg's theory this will take care of itself since students are not usually all on the same stage, and the reasons or considerations offered by those at a higher stage will naturally challenge and attract students at lower stages. It is best, therefore, to avoid attempting to apply the stage theory in too quick or too simple a manner at least until considerable experience in moral discussions is gained.

## NOTES

1. P. McPhail, J. R. Ungoed-Thomas, and H. Chapman, *Moral Education in the Secondary School* (London: Longmans, 1972).
2. See E. Turiel, "An Experimental Test of the Sequentiality of Developmental Stages in the Child's Moral Judgments," *Journal of Personality and Social Psychology* 3 (1966): 611-618; E. Turiel "Developmental Processes in the Child's Moral Thinking," in *Trends and Issues in Developmental Psychology*, ed., P. Mussen, J. Langer, and M. Covington (New York: Holt, Rinehart and Winston, 1969) pp. 93-131; and J. Rest, E. Turiel, and L. Kohlberg, "Levels of Moral Development as a Determinant of Preference and Comprehension of Moral Judgments Made by Others," *Journal of Personality* 37 (1969): 225-252.
3. J. Fletcher, *Situation Ethics* (Philadelphia: Westminster Press, 1966), and J. Fletcher, *Moral Responsibility* (Philadelphia: Westminster Press, 1967).
4. R. E. Galbraith and T. M. Jones, *Teaching Strategies for Moral Dilemmas* (Pittsburgh, Pa.: Social Studies Curriculum Center, Carnegie-Mellon University, 1974).
5. R. E. Galbraith and T. M. Jones, *Instruction for Teaching Moral Dilemmas* (Pittsburgh, Pa.: Social Studies Curriculum Center, Carnegie-Mellon University, 1974).
6. Copyright © 1974 Social Studies Curriculum Center, Carnegie-Mellon University, Pittsburgh, Pennsylvania.

# 9

# From Theory to Practice II: Moral Concept Analysis, Games, and Simulations

## MORAL CONCEPTS: THE ANALYTICAL DISCUSSION METHOD

While the case study is perhaps the best practical method for moral education, it should not be emphasized to the exclusion of other learning activities. A second approach, one easily coordinated with the case study, centers on the analysis of some of the most common concepts or ideas which enter into moral thinking. A moral concept, in this sense, can be either a designation of a specific type of activity, like telling a lie or keeping a promise, or one of the more general notions to which people commonly appeal in talking about their decisions, like friendship, obligation, or conscience.

Our rationale for this approach is rather unsophisticated; it is based on the assumption that when people think about actions, they use these common words or concepts as tools of their decision-making. The more people understand the meanings and implications of these notions, the better they will be able to think. Thus, the effort to develop such understanding is an appropriate goal for moral education.

Our approach here, similar to that of the case study, is toward providing an environment in which young people can have a certain kind of experience or even practice in moral thinking. It is a classroom discussion approach which is "inductive" in the sense of asking students to reflect upon their own experience and to draw generalizations from what they already know.

There are many discussion classes, not all of which are suitable to our purpose. One type, which is sometimes (perhaps mistakenly) called a discussion, is the simple question-and-answer recitation between teacher and students—the "teeth-pulling" type. The students have supposedly prepared an assignment or studied some material which the teacher orally quizzes them about. Considering what we have said about the nature of moral education, however, this type of discussion is undoubtedly to be avoided. It implies that there are right and wrong answers to moral questions and that the teacher is merely attempting to elicit the right ones. Since students often assume that this is the way adults would "teach" morality (and they are quite right), it is especially important to avoid encouraging this assumption and the educational atmosphere it creates.

A second type of discussion is often called "inductive" but is not quite the same as what we have in mind. In this discussion process there is also a right or predetermined answer to the question in the sense that the teacher has a well-formulated content in mind. This is usually a single concept, operation, or understanding which the teacher is trying to help his students grasp. The student, however, is not presumed to have learned the concept before class. The objective is, rather, the development of a concept or perspective which is new to students.

While this type of discussion is possibly more useful in moral education, since we do sometimes wish students to develop new concepts and perspectives, it too is objectionable for our purposes because of its tendency to place the teacher in a position of having the answers or, in this case, the right concept or perspective. In moral education the objective is not the correct answers to particular questions but the development of a better way of thinking. Any discussion which encourages students to think only about "what the teacher wants" serves to thwart the students' own thought and lead moral education away from its real objective. What is usually called "inductive" discussion, therefore, is not quite as open as what we have in mind. One cannot "have a discussion bringing out the following points," as teachers' notes often say, and expect that it will really be an open discussion.

At the opposite extreme is a third common type of classroom discussion in which students are simply encouraged to formulate and express their own opinions. In this discussion, which is often used for sharing opinions about social issues, it is not assumed that there is any single "right" answer for which students are searching. One opinion is as good as the next. This form of discussion is indeed open in the sense we have been suggesting, but it also falls short of our goal by not requiring enough rigorous thought on the part of students. Giving the impression that moral thought is entirely a matter of personal opinion will indeed work against our objective. Differences of opinion are to be both expected and respected, but there is a difference between a well-thought-out moral position and an unconsidered opinion. The kind of discussion that only canvasses opinions can give the impression that any one opinion is as good as the next and that moral decision is, after all, a matter of mere personal opinion or feeling. So, while the openness of the opinion survey discussion is good, more can be done to promote active thought about opinions on the part of students than is ever accomplished by the simple sharing of thoughts and feelings.

In the type of discussion we recommend, therefore, students would be encouraged to formulate and express their own views without feeling that the teacher is looking for a correct answer, but they would also be encouraged to examine their opinions and consider the meanings of the concepts they are using and the ideas to which they appeal. Somewhat like the inductive discussion, it has an overall purpose—the critical examination of opinions, words, and concepts—but it differs from the inductive approach in having no absolutely fixed content. It is free to follow its own development and the students' interests. It is also like the open opinion discussion in that students are encouraged to contribute their own thoughts, say, for example, on what the word "promise" means to them. But it differs from the simple opinion discussion in that it has as its objective the critical examination of a word or concept, the interchange of ideas, and the development of better understanding.

A better idea of a concept analysis discussion might be conveyed by an account of one. After a case study class dealing with a situation in which one person was tempted to avoid an embarrassment by telling a lie, the class was asked to consider what the term "lie" meant. The discussion was proposed because it had become obvious during the previous session that some of the students were trying to win approval of the person telling the lie by arguing that "after all" it was really only a "white" lie and that lies of this sort are quite common. Other students insisted that it was not a "white" lie at all, but a more serious offense of dishonesty.

The teacher began the session by asking what a "white" lie was and how it differed from an ordinary lie. In a relatively short time it was decided that the adjective "white" with its associations of purity and goodness actually only indicated that the person using the phrase approved of that particular lie. It was, in short, a value term, and there was no distinction in fact between white lies and ordinary lies.

After some consideration about the possible implications of red, green, and yellow lies—a digression which, one hopes, may have helped to keep the atmosphere friendly and to encourage students to use their imaginations—the discussion leader asked for an example of a white lie, that is, a lie of which almost anyone would approve. Various suggestions were offered, such as declining an invitation on the grounds that one has a "previous engagement," complimenting a mediocre cook or artist, or telling your grandmother that you like her new hat. In retrospect it seems that at this stage in the discussion most students began to take seriously, although it was not explicitly mentioned, the idea that some lies are acceptable while others are not and that the choice between the two was a personal one. The teacher had indicated his approval of telling a lie in a certain situation but had shown doubts about other cases. A number of students suggested, as cases of which everyone would approve, the telling of lies to parents and to other authority figures. Other students disagreed with these examples. Since it had previously been established that the designation "white lie" was not a factual distinction, however, it now became clearer to students that whether or not a lie is acceptable (morally) is a matter about which people really have to decide for themselves; it is not simply obvious that some lies are "white" and therefore all right, while others are not and are therefore wrong. It may seem to be a small matter, but it is really rather important to moral education to bring students in various ways to the realization that their own actions actually involve decisions—that some things we do almost without a second thought involve choices. Trivial as it may seem, this sort of realization helps to build sensitivity to the moral domain.

After considering various examples of lies of which people normally approve, this particular discussion took a curious turn. Someone had suggested that it was "of course" all right for parents to tell lies to their children as, for example, when they told them about Santa Claus, the Easter Bunny, and the tooth fairy. Discussion then ranged for a time around myths and fairy tales and whether children believed them as literal truth or not. One student said that she had been very upset with her parents for not telling her the truth about Santa Claus when she was young; she eventually found out from her friends and had been embarrassed that everyone knew except her. When another student said that he wondered about his parents telling his little brother that babies were delivered by storks, the discussion took another turn. Deceiving children about Santa Claus and the Easter Bunny might be excused as relatively harmless myth-making, but in this case it seemed to students that the youngster was plainly being given false information when there was no need for it. The pros and cons of telling children about human sexuality were then discussed in a general sort of way, and this produced considerable agreement on one aspect of the issue. Telling children things that are false may at times be necessary, but it does lead youngsters, once they begin to discover the truth, to disbelieve and distrust their parents. This came out in particular when the teacher asked about the case of telling a young child that there was a dragon in the woods that would eat him if he ever went there alone.

A second class session on the topic began roughly where the first one left off. The teacher reviewed the previous conversation, especially the last part, drawing the generalization that one of the consequences of repeated lies and stories to children is that they tend to destroy confidence. This moralism proved to be a false start since it gave both the teacher and the students something of the feeling of an authoritarian classroom. The discussion picked up, however, when a student raised the question of whether an adopted child ought to be told that he is adopted or not. A number of points were made in favor of telling the child at an early age; a few against it. One student said that he was adopted and was happy he had been told about it when he was quite young. Others imagined themselves in his position (note the Golden Rule reasoning) and agreed that if they had been adopted they would definitely want to be told. The teacher asked if they thought that this should apply in all cases, or whether there might be an instance where a youngster ought not to be told. Some thought it should always apply, others thought there might be exceptions; but this line of thought came to a dead end when no one, including the teacher, was able to produce an example of when a child should not to be told.

The question of telling a child he is adopted, however, led the discussion into another area in which concepts and ideas could be clarified. The teacher suggested that the parents of an adopted child could avoid the problem of telling him a lie if the child never happened to ask the question. Reaction to this suggestion was quick: "The parents have an obligation to tell him whether he asks or not." "Withholding information is just like a lie." "They are misleading him if they don't tell." "It is best to tell the child when he is real young, so of course they have to tell him before he could ever ask." This brought out an underlying issue: direct lies are not the only kind of dishonesty one can be involved in, and the fact that a situation does not call for a direct lie does not necessarily excuse a person from responsibility. This point was not so much directly stated as it was implied in a rather rambling discussion about intentionally misleading statements, wrong impressions, encouraging a person's false impressions, withholding information, and the like. There was a good deal of differing opinion on these issues. The question of whether a salesman would be legally guilty or not for not telling the purchaser of a house that it was full of termites was raised. Were this a civics class, the legal question might have been followed up; in this instance it was not, since it would have taken some research to find an answer. The idea that sometimes people have a right to know the truth was mentioned, but it was not followed up analytically, despite one or two probing questions by the teacher.

The discussion of misleading statements and withholding information did, however, lead back to the original question of exactly what constitutes a lie. Students responded with a few simple definitions to which the teacher in turn responded with further questions (trying to get the students to be as precise as possible):

*First Student:* A lie is telling something that's wrong.
*Teacher:* Wrong because the person shouldn't have said it?
*First Student:* No, something that isn't true.
*Teacher:* What if I tell you the earth is flat? That's not true.
*First Student:* It's a lie.
*Second Student:* No it's not; it's just stupid.

*First Student:* Well, if he said it and it wasn't true, it must be a lie.

*Second Student:* But you wouldn't believe him.

*Third Student:* He [the teacher] knows no one would believe him so he couldn't be lying.

*Teacher:* What if I really believed it and wanted to convince you? What if I was Columbus and thought the world was really flat?

*Third Student:* Columbus thought it was round!

*Teacher:* Well, I mean what if I lived before Columbus?

*Second Student:* It's still just stupid. You couldn't make him believe you.

*Third Student:* You can't tell a lie if no one believes you.

*Teacher:* I could try to tell a lie even though no one believed me.

*Teacher:* What if you asked me what time it was and I looked at my watch and told you it was 11:30, but my watch had stopped and it was really 12:15?

*First Student:* Then you are telling a lie.

*Second Student:* No he's not.

*Third Student:* He didn't *know* his watch stopped.

*First Student:* Well, it's wrong, and someone might believe him when he says it.

*Second Student:* He can't tell a lie and not know he's doing it. You have to know it when you're lying.

*Teacher:* If I really believe what I'm saying, it isn't a lie, right?

*Second Student:* Right, you have to know that what you are saying is wrong.

*Teacher:* Wrong, or false?

*Second Student:* False, I guess.

*Teacher:* What if I looked at my watch—this is a puzzle—what if I looked at my watch, and so I really thought it was 11:30, but I wanted to tell you a lie, so I said it was 12:15. But my watch had stopped, and it really was 12:15, so I was actually telling the truth.

With this minor absurdity a number of students responded at once, but since none of them had the attention of the whole group, they simply began speaking to each other in small groups. This can be helpful at times because it gives everyone a chance to speak. In this case the question was a complex one (How could a person be telling a lie and telling the truth at the same time?), and students needed time to explain it to one another and to figure out what they thought. After a short time, when one student thought he had it all figured out, the teacher helped him get the attention of the rest of the class. His account was not directly accepted, but the full class discussion went on until most realized that the person would be lying in the sense of trying to deceive but telling the truth in the sense of making a correct statement.

At this point it seemed time to turn away from analytical questions and back to the moral issue. The teacher did this fairly abruptly with the following case (presented orally):

> Suppose Mary, who is a sophmore in high school, has just recently been getting to know Bill, who is a star on the football team and is class vice-president. The junior prom is about a month away, and she thinks that Bill will probably ask her to go with him. But before he asks, a boy she has known for a long time, John, asks if she will go to the prom with him. Mary has always liked John as a friend—they were neighbors and had always gone to school together—so she doesn't want to hurt his feelings, but she would rather go to the prom with Bill if he asks her. What should she do?

In the discussion that followed, the students mentioned alternatives, most of which involved telling lies, and various unpleasant consequences, but the teacher did not try to formulate their thoughts according to the case study outline, nor did he pursue explicitly the lines of questioning. This happened to be the conclusion of this series of discussion classes. There is, of course, the general problem of working a subject to death, but it might have been profitable to follow up with a case that would raise more general issues of truth in public statements made by a government, such as the following:

> Assume that the United States has a secret missile base in Turkey. If a potential enemy does not know about it, the enemy will not put up a defense against the missiles. But if the enemy finds out about it, the base will be practically useless militarily. If the Senate Foreign Relations Committee is told about the base, it is almost certain that its existence will soon be public knowledge. How should the president or his representative, the secretary of state, respond when the committee members ask him whether there are any bases in Turkey?

The relationship between case studies and analytical discussions is obviously very close. The analytical discussion we have described grew out of a case and led, two sessions later, into another. All things considered, however, there is quite a difference between case studies and analytic discussion, especially from the perspective of the discussion leader. In a case study the object is to consider the alternatives, the consequences, the reasons for and against decisions, and make a judgment on the question. In an analytic discussion the object is to consider some general concept such as telling lies in order to reach a better understanding, not a single opinion or judgment. Case study seems most productive if the teacher tries to keep to the issue, sometimes, for example, by keeping a blackboard list of alternative actions and consequences and by working through the philosophical lines of questioning outlined above. The case study is by nature inclined to raise many different ideas and opinions, and the discussion leader has the task of bringing some order out of the various responses and reactions. In an analytical discussion the facilitator's task is almost the opposite: he is attempting to bring students to imagine different instances, to look at the concept from various angles, and to develop perceptive understanding.

In this kind of discussion we occasionally have also dealt with practical problems of immediate concern to students such as the use of drugs. But here, as we noted earlier with the case studies, the topic is inclined to be too close, too real, too emotional for students to be able to treat analytically. Helping students to deal with their own immediate problems is certainly an admirable objective for moral education, but it is a little beyond what we are fully prepared to deal with at this point. We have found that students do appreciate discussions of these problems, and it is perhaps beneficial to enter into one of these areas from time to time as any good teacher will when an issue is really troubling students. This can help to keep the atmosphere real by demonstrating to students that moral education ultimately deals with important issues. We have found that when students learn some of the techniques of moral thinking (looking for the alternatives, consequences, and so on), they are at times able to apply these to their own immediate problems. But this success, minor as it has been, is probably more of a product of the discussion atmosphere established earlier in talking about less volatile issues and not the point at which moral education should begin. We try, therefore, to deal with issues of immediate concern only when students raise them (though with some classes this is too often), not because giving young people help with their problems is not a valid objective, but simply because moral education as the development of decision-making abilities has not yet advanced to the level of complexity to deal very creatively with these concerns.

Exactly what words or concepts might be up for discussion depends very much upon the students. It would do little good to center on sophisticated moral notions or value concepts to which students are unaccustomed; it is not a question of teaching new ideas. The objective is, rather, to build insight into and understanding of the concepts students already know and use. Telling lies is only one example, of course; we have done much the same with the question of making and breaking promises, friendship and loyalty, courage, responsibility, cheating, and conscience. Working a good discussion on any of these topics may, of course, require some preparation on the part of the teacher. Since most of us are rather vague in our own understanding of these notions, the analytical discussion should be prepared in a general way by sharpening one's own concepts and ideas. But this does not involve bringing any new content to the class other than our personal experience and understanding.

A schematic outline of a type teachers might use for analysis of thinking skills involved in this discussion would include:

> Definition—what is a lie?
> Differentiation—between types of lies, facts, and values.
> Grouping—similar types of lies.
> Classification—in terms of motives and consequences.
> Ordering—which is more important?

Additional differentiation and grouping:

> Testing—looking for contrary cases.
> Predicting—the consequences of lies.
> Generalizing—similar cases require similar judgments.

Teaching materials for the organization of this type of analysis would include:

> Content analysis—various definitions and differentiations of the concept.

Hypothetical cases.
Role play.
Discussion focus statements.
Diagrams of alternative strategies.
Theoretical statements of various positions or principles (characterizations of philosophical positions).

## GAMES AND SIMULATIONS

Finally, although experience with this technique is more recent and less extensive than with case discussions, we should like to say something about the use of games and simulations in moral education. Games can provide a most important supplement to other moral education learning activities, for they permit us to deal not only with the decisions people think they should make, as in discussing hypothetical cases, but also with people's actual choices and reactions. This point was made quite clearly in the script of a recent British Broadcasting Corporation program on educational games:

> At first glance it may appear that discussion should be an adequate way of handling moral education, but experience has shown that discussion alone often does not result in involvement or identification. Furthermore, verbal statements are frequently notoriously dishonest. When a boy or girl is asked to state what he or she would do in a given situation the immediate tendency is to give a high status answer popular with teachers or parents, to be as the Scots say, "unco guid"—too good to be true. The inclination is not to say what one *would* do but rather what one *ought* to do—to demonstrate the "right" answer as far as that is recognized. Unless you think moral education is only education in the theory of moral decision taking this will not satisfy you. . . . If you want to work on attitude and behavior change developed as a result of greater insight and rational autonomy you must start by being honest, and the use of role play is an aid to honesty.[1]

The basic purpose of educational games is, thus, to provide a direct experience of decision-making. They can make students aware of the actual pressures arising in situations requiring decisions and can counteract the tendency to eliminate or neglect real feelings and reactions in hypothetical discussions.

Having the kinds of experiences that educational games can produce, however, is not alone sufficient. Games really provide only the raw material for education; whether a direct experience is educational or not depends very much upon what is done with it later. Some people seem to profit by their experience almost automatically, but others, perhaps the majority of us, only profit from experience if we take time to reflect upon it later. This point was especially emphasized by one consultant, Mr. Pat Tansey, on the BBC series just mentioned. "The post-play discussion," he said, "is of vital importance to the learning process for it is at this point that the attention of the players is directed toward the pre-determined educational objectives of the game."[2] The purpose of a game as a learning activity, therefore, is basically to provide direct experience of a kind which can be used as the basis of later reflection. Both the experience and the later reflection can be educative. If one learns by experience, as is often said, then having an experience designed to illustrate particular aspects of life can be an effective way of learning, and because one also profits from his experience when he reflects upon it and develops new insights, discussion of the game experience is an important part of learning technique.

Perhaps the most common classroom game is the role play. Many teachers indeed use this technique either as a discussion starter or even within a discussion to bring out people's actual feelings or to elicit empathy for a person in a certain situation. It can easily be coordinated with the case study method and with the analytical discussion. For example, parts of the case of the neighborhood storekeeper could be played out, such as a scene in which the storekeeper tries to explain the situation to one of the youngsters' parents. Alternative scenes could then be played by assuming, for example, that the parent is defensive, hostile, or extremely embarrassed when the storekeeper confronts him. Or role play could have been used at the end of the analytical discussion described above in the case of the high school girl and the choice of dates for the prom. In this case a role play could certainly have fulfilled the function mentioned above because the discussion really had neglected or tended to play down the actual force of the temptation to tell a lie in a situation where one's better judgment may have been against it. If through a simulation, the students could have been brought to experience the actual pressure of the temptation, they could have dealt more fully with it. Becoming aware of one's own feelings is an important aspect of moral education and one for which role play is a far better learning activity than an ordinary discussion.

Conducting role play in the classroom is not as easy as one might expect. Although one does not have to be a born actor to use this learning activity successfully, role play does require a bit of skill. The necessary abilities can be learned, however, by both teachers and students if, as with discussion skills, some attention is paid to the process. Even students and teachers with a natural flair for acting need to adapt their skills to the particular requirements of the classroom role play. One cannot expect to take a class that has never engaged in a role play and have them immediately improvise a scene. Roles may have to be described rather fully and precisely at first, and some cues on lines or time for private rehearsal of one's role may need to be given. Immediate role interaction is the objective, but few of us are ready for this without previous experience. Advice about role play is readily available. It is a learning activity for which some preparation is required and at which teachers develop skill only with experience, but it is worth the effort.

Other games and simulation exercises are more elaborate, take more class time, and provide better interaction. Most also require less individual skill than role play. While it is not always possible to arrange time and space for more elaborate games in the normal school curriculum, the effort is definitely worth it. Simulations and games do not have to be used terribly often to be effective. One game can provide experience that will be useful in different ways throughout a term; two or three games over a year's time can add a whole new dimension to almost any course.

Games can do many different things for classes, and it is impossible to describe their potential in general terms. The best we can do is to offer an account of a few games which we have found especially suited to moral education and hope that it will encourage the reader to explore this area for himself.

*The Marriage Game* is a simulation which puts students in the situation of young people.[3] While the immediate subject of the game is the marital relationship, however, its emphasis is on the decisions young married people face, as is indicated in its subtitle "Understanding Marital Decision-Making," and it is thus an appropriate exercise for moral education among, for example, high school seniors.

In the strict sense a simulation is a game which is modeled on certain aspects of real life. *The Marriage Game* has many such facets: players make basic decisions concerning jobs, leisure time, finances, housing, and so on; they many enter into relationships (marriage, joint housing arrangements) or break them off (divorce). In each case their decisions have definite consequences: for example, a man who works two jobs has a higher income but loses a certain amount of freedom and esteem.

In addition to the fixed consequences of decisions which are clearly indicated to the participants before they make their decisions, there are certain chance effects which are closely modeled on real life. These chance effects are determined by cards which reflect the possible consequences of decisions that the participant makes. After a person chooses a job, for example, there is a 6 percent chance determined by a chance-card drawing that he will lose it and be unemployed for part of the round. There is also a 2 percent chance that he will have to go to the hospital for an operation, in which case he must pay certain costs not covered by insurance and he loses both freedom and sexual gratification. Sexual gratification, obtained by exchanging cards, also involves some real life contingencies: if players do not purchase contraceptives, probability of pregnancy is determined according to the number of cards exchanged, or if sexual gratification cards are exchanged with anyone other than a person's spouse, there is a 5 percent chance per partner of contracting a venereal disease. All in all, the contingencies, both fixed and chance, are as close to real life as possible: a used car, for example, costs much less than a new compact car or a luxury car, but it brings less esteem and must be junked after two years.

Of particular interest to the moral educator is the manner in which the overall outcome of a round of decisions (simulating one year) is calculated. At the outset of the game students are asked to state some of their values or priorities from a given list which includes such things as freedom, security, esteem, and enjoyment. The game is not one of competition. At the end of each round points are calculated to determine the extent to which each player's decisions promoted or impeded the values he had adopted. Players do not win or lose in the *Marriage Game* but are given a rough indication of the degree to which their decision-making correlates with their stated values. If this "marital satisfaction score," as it is called, is low for one round, the player will see that his decisions are not promoting the kind of life he thinks he wants. In succeeding rounds he may either change his values or his decisions. As a simulation *The Marriage Game* creates in play-practice decision situations similar to those in which we have attempted to place students in case study and analytical discussions.

There are many games available now that deal with values and value clarification, some of which can be quite useful in moral education. One such game, *Valuing Simulation*, requires participants to choose value statements (some of which are stated in religious language) with which they agree and then to form "communities" of people who share similar values.[4] Students come to analyze the value statements they have adopted when they try to discover the essential characteristics of their communal consensus and attempt to tell others what commonality holds their group together. In a later phase of the game participants discuss their chosen values with others who have adopted opposite views. As an experience in "synthesizing and synergizing," participants attempt to come to an agreement on a new value statement to which both can give assent.

Unlike some value games *Valuing Simulation* treats valuing as a process. It emphasizes exploring the consequences associated with various options, interpreting the meanings of various value statements to others, discovering areas of coherence and inconsistency in different combinations or sets of values, and attempting to bring some form of tolerable harmony out of initially opposing positions. It is thus quite consistent with our view of developing moral principles and values out of individual decisions.

Although value games can indeed be useful at certain points in moral education, they must be used cautiously. First, values are sometimes treated as fixed entities, almost as objects which a person possesses. In those learning activities which promote this view the participant may not experience the process of developing his own values. Values may in fact be presented almost as objects for sale, giving the "supermarket" impression which Alvin Toffler believes will come to replace personal development and creativity.

Second, we have reservations about value games because they often seem to put the cart before the horse. Participants are inclined to get the impression that one must *first* choose his values in an abstract sort of way and *then* make his moral decision. As our presentation of the philosophical approach to morality attempted to demonstrate, however, moral principles and values are best thought of as implied in, or underlying, decisions; they can be made by conscious reflection but are seldom adopted in the abstract. It is because of this perspective that we have spoken of moral education more as decision-making than as a question of values. Values and value education are all the fad lately; we may even develop young people who are quite articulate about their values but still can't make decisions.

*Human Relations*[5] is a game that we have used with high school juniors and seniors, with college students, and with adults. The experience it provides focuses on the problem of cooperation and competition. In this game the group is initially divided into two teams (of no more than twelve to fifteen members each—others can act as observers) which meet and remain in separate rooms throughout the game. They interact only through their representatives and the judge (usually the teacher), who at times can play an active part in influencing the course of events through his decisions. The players are given copies of the rules, as follows, from which they discover the objectives of the game and the moves open to them. They do not usually understand the rules very well until the first few moves are completed, but they should go ahead anyway.

## HUMAN RELATIONS GAME RULES

1.  Each team elects a chairman, two negotiators, a messenger, and a recorder.
2.  Each team is given twelve ordinary playing cards, face down.
3.  After the initial planning period teams will have five minutes between moves (the time may later be shortened or extended by the judge). Teams may be penalized by the judge for delays.
4.  At each move each team may turn one or two cards up, one or two cards down (if they previously had any up), or leave their cards as they are.
5.  At the end of each five-minute decision period, or at whatever previous time they may choose, the messenger must report the move to the judge in writing. No changes are allowed if the report is submitted early.
6.  At the beginning of the game each team has thirty chips, and an additional thirty are held by the judge in the "bank."
7.  The first team to have all its cards turned up may claim the "bank."
8.  At any move, either team may challenge the other. At this point the team with the most cards turned up (whichever team it is) must pay the other team one chip for each card it has turned up more than the upturned cards of the other team. Any challenge must be clearly indicated on the messenger's report and will be calculated after the turning of cards for that move. After a challenge all cards are again turned down. (Only at the time of a challenge will teams know how many cards the other team has turned up.)

9. Negotiation takes place when one team calls for it and the other team agrees to it, or when they mutually agree. A team may call for negotiation at any move. Each team must signify with each move whether it calls for negotiation, is willing to negotiate, or is unwilling to negotiate. Negotiation takes place before the judge, who sets the time for it. Teams must be willing to negotiate after every third move if the other team calls for it. The judge may call a negotiation at any time.

10. The object of the game is to finish with more chips than you began.

11. The game is over when either team claims the "bank," when either team loses all its chips, or when the game is terminated by the judge.

From reading these rules the players do *not* usually form any immediate impression of what the game is like. In fact, the rules simply set up the conditions of interaction, conditions with a built-in ambiguity and a nearly unresolvable conflict or competition situation. What happens during play depends entirely upon the participants. Leadership evolves in each team but often changes if it seems that little or no progress is being made. The teams often develop mistaken or fanciful impressions of each other; often there are efforts at deceit and usually a good deal of frustration when players begin to feel that they cannot attain their objective. It normally takes two to three hours to play the game (without the discussion), but it can go on almost indefinitely. In the twenty-five or thirty times we have used this game the outcome has never been the same. At best we can give only a few random comments here on some of the more typical events.

First, although *Human Relations* may appear to be a game of simple competition, it is not. Any strategy that one side takes can be countered by the other team. This means that the whole atmosphere is not what one would ordinarily expect from a game. Often a stalemate develops in which the participants become frustrated, although unwilling to concede defeat to the other team. The emotions students feel at this point are important; they are generally competitive and frustrated at the same time and often later come to realize the influence of these feelings on their thoughts and actions.

As the game continues, it soon becomes obvious that since neither side can do much on its own, some form of cooperation must be arranged. Negotiation is attempted, but the rules give no guidance for reaching agreement. The negotiation process creates a second, personal, conflict of attempting to cooperate, which requires some form of trust with the very people one eventually hopes to outwit.

Another aspect of the game is the dynamics of the interaction. Since each team must choose its own leaders, the normal problems of leadership ensue, especially when the leaders are unable to come up with a winning strategy. The negotiation is another field of interaction; usually a bargain of some sort develops in which one team promises to give or pay a certain amount if the other makes certain moves. This raises the question of trusting the other team to keep its promise. Interaction and negotiation often center on deceit, broken promises, and attempted trickery. Players are caught between the desire to trust and cooperate with the other team and their own fears of being taken.

The outcome of the game is nearly always different. In fact, it is not the sort of game in which one team must win and the other must lose. *Both* teams *can* attain the objective of having more chips than they began with. The only way this can happen, however, is for one or both to claim the bank. (In our experience this has never happened.) Often one team gets a few chips ahead of the other on the first or second move, but its members soon realize that just being ahead does not count for much since it is unable to terminate the game. Sometimes a few players realize that both teams can actually win the game, but they are usually unable to convince the others and almost never able to get all to trust each other enough to conclude the game successfully in this way. When they later realize that both teams could have won if they had only had enough trust and understanding, unexpected and perceptive insights into human relations often develop. Participants realize often the extent to which they were hampered by their own preconceived ideas and emotions.

Postgame discussion is important, but students often get too involved to be able to look clearly at their own emotions immediately. Over the course of a week or so, however, they can examine the feelings and thoughts they had during the game and look at their decisions and actions. Exactly what participants learn depends upon the dynamics of the group. It must be remembered that participants have different roles in the game, and they bring different personalities to it, so it should be expected that they will learn different things about themselves and their decisions. The best kind of postgame discussion usually centers on the question of what was influencing people to feel and act as they did.

The relationship of the learning experience provided by *Human Relations* to the objectives of moral education is fairly direct. Students have the opportunity to reflect on the factors that influence their decisions; they are forced to calculate the effects of their actions on others and to attempt to interpret the actions of others. Insights are developed into the dynamics of communication (which often breaks down) and into the importance of communication in solving social problems.

## NOTES

1. *Games and Simulations,* (London: British Broadcasting Corporation, 1973), p. 34.

2. *Games and Simulations*, p. 5.

3. C. S. Greenblatt, P. J. Stein, and N. F. Washburne, *The Marriage Game: Understanding Marital Decision-Making.* New York: Random House, 1974.

4. *Valuing Simulation*, Mobley and Associates, 5000 Sheppard Lane, Endicott City, Maryland, 21043.

5. Source unknown.

# 10

# Conclusion: Five Theses on Moral Education

In the foregoing chapters we outlined a general proposal for the theory and practice of moral education. On the theoretical side it included several basic perspectives: (1) a principle of education without indoctrination, (2) a philosophical analysis of the nature of moral judgment, and (3) psychological analyses of moral development both in thought processes and in personality. On the practical side our proposal included the establishment of a classroom atmosphere in which moral development can be facilitated through both experience in decision-making and practice in the skills of moral reasoning.

To summarize our proposal more fully than this would seem redundant: our presentation was a cumulative one, so there is really nothing to be "brought together" in conclusion. At least we hope that what we have been up to has not been a mystery. It might be helpful, however, if we conclude by stating as directly as possible what we take to be the most promi-

171

nent characteristics of our approach; and we would like to add a comment or two on each.

Our proposal for the theory and practice of moral education can be comprehended under the following five theses:

## I. Moral Education Should Avoid Indoctrinating Individuals into any System of Values or Beliefs.

Not only should educators in a free society avoid teaching any single system of moral principles or beliefs, but they should also avoid, as we insisted in considering the affective aspects of moral development, the inculcation of attitudes, habits, or patterns of behavior. Moral education can and should be undertaken in a free society only as a matter of attempting to give students the skills and abilities of moral decision-making so that they may develop their own moral perspectives through interactive experience. We *can* teach students that people do act for moral reasons and that this is an important aspect of human behavior because it enters into the whole constitution of one's lifestyle. The principles and ideals people adopt ultimately determine the kinds of people they are and will be, so being cognizant of the moral domain is one way of being better able to govern the course of one's own life.

But teaching the skills of moral thought and giving experience in decision-making are not the same as insisting that students adopt any particular perspective; nor, for that matter, is it the same as *insisting* that they adopt a moral perspective at all. The line should be drawn between giving young people the skills and abilities to think morally, along with some practical experience in this domain on the one hand, and aiming at behavioral or attitudinal changes on the other.

On the issue of influencing students' behavior moral education is really in no different a position than education in other fields. The mathematics teacher, for example, teaches the skills of mathematical calculation but does not attempt to inculcate any particular "mathematical" behavioral pattern or attitude. To expect that moral education will change the behavior or the attitudes of students is an unacceptable way to formulate our objectives. We should aim only at giving students the skills and abilities to make moral decisions. We hope, of course, that students will go on to use their acquired skills and accumulated experience in making their own decisions, just as the mathematics teacher would hope that students find mathematical skills useful. And, of course, if students never found either of these sets of skills useful, we would say that something is wrong. But to insist that students develop a behavioral pattern or attitude of using them, or that moral education should in this sense make students more moral (more capable, yes; more moral, not necessarily) goes beyond what we feel to be the legitimate objectives of public education.

## II. Moral Judgment Constitutes a Particular Identifiable Form of Rational Thought.

The theory of moral education presented here stands in contrast to many other proposals—certainly to some of the most popular ones in the United States—in that it has a definite philosophical focus. This is a perspective originally proposed for moral education by Mr. John Wilson, but one which has been unfortunately neglected as interest in psychological theories has arisen. The moral domain, as we see it, is *not* a realm in which human thought and action are generated by psychosocial stages of development or cognitive-structural orientations in such a way that conscious thought (decision-making) is really insignificant. Moral decision-making is, or at least at best can be, an intellectual process: reasons are not the only motives for actions, but they are motives—important ones. We are convinced, therefore, that the moral domain must be treated as a domain of rational thought as well as one of psychosocial development.

Adopting a philosophical perspective has not, however, required us to give up our criterion of nonindoctrination. We have not proposed the teaching of any particular theory of morality such as natural law, utilitarianism, or Professor Rawls's theory of justice. Philosophical analysis has provided us with a description of what constitutes a moral judgment irrespective of any particular theory of morality, inasmuch as this is possible. This analysis has been translated into various lines of "Socratic" questioning by which one can determine whether any particular decision and its attendant reasons are, in fact, moral. In contrast both to proposals for the teaching of a particular set of moral values and to proposals limited to the indirect facilitation of moral development through the stages of maturation, therefore, we have proposed the more or less direct teaching of some of the skills of moral reasoning.

### III. Moral Development Takes Place Through a Series of Cognitive Stages.

On this point we are in agreement with many researchers and theorists in the field. Moral development is a natural maturational process, but one which can be impeded or even thwarted by environmental conditions. Our proposal for moral education is based upon the supposition, for which we find substantial evidence, that educators can facilitate moral growth by providing an environment which supports and encourages this development—a microcosm, so to speak, for the fertilization and gestation of higher levels of thought.

There is, furthermore, one other point arising from this thesis on which there is considerable agreement among moral educators. Even if regular moral education classes were established in schools and were generally successful in creating the desired environment, the effort would still only constitute a microcosmic and in many respects an artificial world of experience. It must be recognized, however, that the everyday home school environment in which young people live is the real moral education environment and that it has, in terms of both time and reality, a greater influence upon them than the small world of the moral education classroom could ever have. Unfortunately, the everyday world is not always an environment which promotes mature moral thinking. It may be, and indeed often is, an environment which impedes, an environment in which social relations are at or even below the students' current stage of development and which, therefore, makes that stage a very difficult one to transcend. To put it more directly, it is difficult to facilitate higher stage development in schools that have institutionalized a stage two standard of interaction—reward and punishment with backscratching. And the reward and punishment syndrome is, unfortunately, the dominant modus operandi in many secondary schools. Creating an effective moral education program may thus require opening the whole school to a recognition of the rights of individuals (teachers as well as students) and to a more democratic process of decision-making. To put the same point philosophically, one can hardly teach the skills of rational moral thought with much effectiveness in a school in which the authority structures are impervious to rational argument, where the powers-that-be are unwilling to consider decisions openly and rationally because they are unable morally to justify their protection of vested interests (backscratching).

IV. Moral Education as the Facilitation of Human Development is Possible Through Giving Individuals Concrete Experience in Decision-Making and Practice in the Skills of Moral Reasoning.

We do not need to summarize what we have said about the practice of moral education in case studies, discussions, and educational games. We have not, however, said anything directly about our view of the place of moral education in the curriculum. This was intentional. If the reader gathered the impression that we were talking about moral education as a whole new subject, that is all right. We do feel that the best way to begin thinking about moral education is to consider it a separate field so that its aims and goals can be established free of the influence of other fields. In theory, moral education is not a part of any other field. In practice, moral education may well be undertaken as an integral part of other subjects such as history, literature, civics, and sociology.

The question of whether specific moral education classes ought to be set up or not will no doubt be debated for a good while. Although we have found that moral education can be successfully integrated into other fields and believe that any decision of this sort will have to be made situationally, there are at least two advantages to treating it as a separate subject. First, when moral education is combined with other subjects, it necessarily inherits the course's structure and class atmosphere. What we have spoken of as the atmosphere of openness and realness necessary to moral education may not be attainable in a course which is under the burden of specific content requirements and a grading system. It may, therefore, be easier to establish the necessary atmosphere if moral education is separated, especially so that it can be made clear to students that there are no absolutely right and wrong answers in this domain and that they are not to be graded on their moral opinions. Second, it may be preferable to conduct moral education as a separate subject for reasons of school-community relations. If it is an elective course rather than part of a required course (at least when first instituted), objections of forcing morality on students may be avoided.

V. Moral Development Can Be Facilitated Only in an Atmosphere of Openness and Personal Integrity.

Finally, and even more intensely than with efforts to democratize the school, the revolution of humanizing the classroom will undoubtedly meet with counterrevolutionary forces. It is difficult to know what advice to give to teachers who want to begin being honest with and respectful of their students. By insisting upon "realness" in the moral education classroom we have indeed asked the moral education teacher to violate some of the most sacred taboos of professionalized teaching; we hardly need to warn anyone with any experience in the schools that being an open teacher is not always popular. We are forced by the nature of the task, however, to ask the prospective moral education teacher where his commitments lie and whether he is willing to take a stand or not against the facades of false professionalism so often presented to students. We must indeed say that if a person is not willing to make an effort at humanizing the classroom, he will hardly make a good moral education teacher. We have never said that the moral education teacher has to be himself a paragon of virtue, but one can hardly ask students to be open and honest about their thoughts if he is unwilling to break down the facade that covers his own social interaction. This is, however, a difficult demand. Much as we might insist that there is no room for weaklings in the revolution, we also realize that much can be accomplished through compromise and persuasion. The effort to help people attain better lives for themselves through moral education is nevertheless something of a revolutionary force in its demand for openness and honesty. Those who join the movement must be warned of its dangers. To them we can only say, May you follow the spirit of Socrates—and avoid his fate.

# Bibliography

## I. INDOCTRINATION

A. General:

Gatchel, R. H. "Evolution of the Concepts of Indoctrination in American Education." *Educational Forum* 23 (March 1959): 303-309.
Snook, I. A. *Concepts of Indoctrination.* London: Routledge and Kegan Paul, 1972.
————. *Indoctrination and Education.* London: Routledge and Kegan Paul, 1972.
————. "The Concept of Indoctrination." *Studies in Philosophy and Education* 7 (Fall 1970): 67-108.

B. Current discussion aimed at an analysis of the concept of indoctrination began with the following two essays:

Hare, Richard M. "Adolescents into Adults." In *Aims in Education.* Edited by T. H. B. Hollins. Manchester, England: Manchester University Press, 1964, pp. 47-70.
Wilson, John. "Education and Indoctrination." In *Aims in Education.* Edited by T. H. B. Hollins. Manchester, England: Manchester University Press, 1964, pp. 24-46.

C. These essays prompted a series of articles, the most important of which are the following (excerpts of each are found in Snook, *Concepts of Indoctrination*):

Atkinson, R. F. "Instruction and Indoctrination." In *Philosophical Analysis and Education.* Edited by R. D. Archambault. London: Routledge and Kegan Paul, 1965, pp. 171-86.
Crittenden, B. "Teaching, Educating, and Indoctrinating." *Educational Theory* 18 (Summer 1968): 237-52.

Flew, Antony. "What is Indoctrination?" *Studies in Philosophy and Education* 4 (Spring 1966): 273-83.
Gregory, I. M. M., and Woods, R. G. "Indoctrination." *Proceedings of the Philosophy of Education Society of Great Britain* 4 (January 1970).
White, J. P. "Indoctrination." In *The Concept of Education*. Edited by R. S. Peters. London: Routledge and Kegan Paul, 1967, pp. 177-91.

D. Other resources on the topic are:

Eckstein, J. "Is It Possible for Schools to be Neutral?" *Educational Theory* 19 (Fall 1969): 337-46.
Ennis, R. H. "The Possibility of Neutrality." *Educational Theory* 19 (Fall 1969): 347-56.
Green, T. F. "A Typology of the Teaching Concept." *Studies in Philosophy and Education* 3 (Winter 1964-65): 284-319.
Gribble, J. *Introduction to Philosophy of Education*. Boston: Allyn and Bacon, 1969.
Kilpatrick, W. H. *Philosophy of Education*. New York: Macmillan, 1951.
McGlucken, W. I. *The Catholic Way in Education*. Milwaukee: Bruce Publishing Co., 1937.
Moore, W. "Indoctrination as a Normative Conception." *Studies in Philosophy and Education* 4 (Summer 1966): 396-403.
Pincoffs, E. L. "On Avoiding Moral Indoctrination." In *Educational Judgments*. Edited by J. F. Doyle. London: Routledge and Kegan Paul, 1973, pp. 59-73.
Pittenger, B. F. *Indoctrination for American Democracy*. New York: Macmillan, 1941.
Wilson, John. "Comments on Flew's 'What is Indoctrination?'" *Studies in Philosophy and Education* 4 (Summer 1966): 390-95.

## II. MORAL EDUCATION

A. The Farmington-Trust research:

Wilson, John. *Practical Methods of Moral Education*. London: Heinemann Educational Books, 1972.
———. *Education in Religion and the Emotions*. London: Heinemann Educational Books, 1971.
Wilson, John.; Williams, N.; and Sugarman, B. *Introduction to Moral Education*. London: Penguin, 1968.

B. The Schools-Council Project:

McPhail, P.; Ungoed-Thomas, J. R.; and Chapman, H. *Moral Education in the Secondary School.* London: Longmans, 1972.

C. Professor Lawrence Kohlberg on education (Kohlberg's psychological research publications are listed below in section IV, D)

Kohlberg Lawrence. "Moral Development and the New Social Studies." *Social Education* 37 (May 1973): 369-75.
———. "Indoctrination Versus Relativity in Value Education." *Zygon* 6 (December 1971).
———. "Education for Justice: A Modern Statement of the Platonic View." In *Moral Education.* Edited by N. F. Sizer and T. R. Sizer. Cambridge, Mass.: Harvard University Press, 1970, pp. 56-83.
———. "Moral Development and the Education of Adolescents." In *Adolescents and the American High School.* Edited by R. Purnell. New York: Holt, Rinehart and Winston, 1970, pp. 144-63.
. "Moral Education in the Schools: A Developmental View." *The School Review* 74 (1966): 1-30.
Kohlberg, L., and Turiel, E. "Moral Development and Moral Education." *Psychology and Educational Practice.* Edited by G. Lesser. Chicago: Scott, Foresman, 1971, pp. 410-65.

D. General:

Beck, Clive M.; Crittenden, B. S.; and Sullivan, E. V. *Moral Education: Interdisciplinary Approaches.* Toronto: University of Toronto Press, 1971.
Bull, Norman J. *Moral Education.* London: Routledge and Kegan Paul, 1969.
Dewey, John. *Moral Principles in Education.* Boston: Houghton Mifflin, 1909.
*Humanist, The.* Moral-Education-for-Children Issue. November/December 1972.
May, P. R. *Moral Education in School.* London: Methuen, 1971.
Miblett, W. R. *Moral Education in a Changing Society.* London: Farber, 1963.
Peters, Richard S. "Moral Education and the Psychology of Character." In *Philosophy and Education.* Edited by I. Scheffler. Boston: Allyn and Bacon, 1966, pp. 263-86.
Sizer, N. F., and Sizer, T. R. *Moral Education.* Cambridge, Mass.: Harvard University Press, 1970.

## III. MORAL PHILOSOPHY

A. The one good anthology for the definition of the term "moral" is:

Wallace, G., and Walker, A. D. M., eds. *The Definition of Morality.* London: Methuen, 1970.

B. Among the best general introductions to moral philosophy are the following:

Aristotle. *Nicomachean Ethics*. Baltimore, Md.: Penguin, 1953.
Atkinson, R. F. *Conduct*. London: Macmillan, 1969.
Baier, Kurt. *The Moral Point of View*. Ithaca, N.Y.: Cornell University Press, 1958.
Frankena, William K. *Ethics*. Englewood Cliffs, N.J.: Prentice-Hall, 1963.
Hudson, W. D. *Modern Moral Philosophy*. Garden City, N.Y.: Doubleday, 1970.
Nowell-Smith, P. H. *Ethics*. Baltimore, Md.: Penguin, 1954.

C. While there is no single source that would provide an account of the nature of moral judgment corresponding directly to our analysis, our approach has been influenced most heavily by the following:

Hare, R. M. *Freedom and Reason*. Oxford: Oxford University Press, 1963.
———. *The Language of Morals*. Oxford: Oxford University Press, 1952.
Rawls, John A. *Theory of Justice*. Cambridge, Mass.: Harvard University Press, 1971.
Toulmin, Stephen. *An Examination of the Place of Reason in Ethics*. Cambridge: At the University Press, 1950.
Warnock, Geoffrey J. *The Object of Morality*. London: Methuen, 1971.

D. Existentialist views:

Kierkegaard, Soren. *Fear and Trembling*. Garden City, N.Y.: Doubleday, 1953.
Sartre, Jean-Paul. "Existentialism is a Humanism." In *Existentialism from Dostoevsky to Sartre*. Edited by W. Kaufmann. New York: World Publishing Co., 1956.

E. Christian ethics:

Fletcher, Joseph F. *Moral Responsibility*. Philadelphia: Westminster Press, 1967.
———. *Situation Ethics*. Philadelphia: Westminster Press, 1966.
Niebuhr, H. Richard. *The Responsible Self*. New York: Harper and Row, 1963.
Ramsey, Paul. *Basic Christian Ethics*. New York: Scribner's, 1950.
Tillich, Paul. *Morality and Beyond*. New York: Harper and Row, 1963.

F. Jewish ethics:

Herberg, Will. *Judaism and Modern Man*. New York: Meridian Books, 1959.
Steinberg, M. *Basic Judaism*. New York: Harcourt, Brace, 1947.

G. General works in the related area of value theory:

Baier, Kurt. "What is Value? An Analysis of the Concept." In *Values and the Future.* Edited by K. Baier and N. Rescher. New York: The Free Press, 1969, pp. 36-67.

Perry, Ralph B. *General Theory of Values.* Cambridge, Mass.: Harvard University Press, 1926.

Rescher, Nicholas. *Introduction to Value Theory.* Englewood Cliffs, N.J.: Prentice-Hall, 1969.


## IV. THE PSYCHOLOGY OF MORAL DEVELOPMENT

A. Psychoanalytic theories:

Erikson, Erik. "Identity and the Life Cycle." *Psychological Issues* 1 (1959): 18-164.
———. *Childhood and Society.* New York: Norton, 1950.

Evans, R. I. *Dialogue with Erik Erikson.* New York: Dutton, 1969.

Freud, Sigmund. *New Introductory Lectures on Psychoanalysis.* New York: Hogarth Press, 1933.

Hall, Calvin. *A Primer of Freudian Psychology.* Cleveland, Ohio: World Publishing Co., 1954.

Nass, M. L. "The Superego and Moral Development in the Theories of Freud and Piaget." *The Psychoanalytic Study of the Child* 21 (1966): 51-68.

Peters, Richard S. "Freud's Theory of Moral Development in Relation to Piaget's." *British Journal of Educational Psychology* 30 (1960): 250-58.

B. Behavioral and social-learning theories:

Aronfreed, J. "The Concept of Internalization." In *Handbook of Socialization Theory and Research.* Edited by D. A. Goslin. Chicago: Rand McNally, 1969, pp. 263-24.
———. *Conduct and Conscience.* New York: Academic Press, 1968.

Bandura, Albert. "Social Learning of Moral Judgments." *Journal of Personality and Social Psychology* 11 (1969): 275-79.

Bandura, A., and McDonald, F. J. "The Influence of Social Reinforcement and the Behavior of Models in Shaping Children's Moral Judgment." *Journal of Abnormal and Social Psychology* 67 (1963): 274-81.

Bandura, A., and Walters, R. H. *Social Learning and Personality Development.* New York: Holt, Rinehart and Winston, 1963.

Eysenck, H. J. *Crime and Personality.* London: Routledge and Kegan Paul, 1964.
———. "The Development of Moral Values in Children." *British Journal of Educational Psychology* 30 (1960): 11-21.

Johnson, R. C.; Ackerman, J. M.; and Frank, H. "Resistance to Temptation, Guilt

Following Yielding, and Psychopathology." *Journal of Consulting and Clinical Psychology* 32 (1968): 169-75.
Johnson, R. C., and Kalafat, J. D. "Projective and Sociometric Measures of Conscience Development." *Child Development* 40 (1969): 651-55.


C. Piaget and related works:

Bloom, L. "Piaget's Theory of the Development of Moral Judgments." *Journal of Genetic Psychology* 95 (1959): 3-12.
Durkin, D. "Children's Concepts of Justice: A Comparison with the Piaget Data." *Child Development* 30 (1959): 59-67.
————. "Children's Concepts of Justice: A Further Comparison with the Piaget Data." *Journal of Educational Research* 52 (1959): 252-57.
Flavell, J. H. *The Developmental Psychology of Jean Piaget.* New York: Van Nostrand, 1963.
Loughran, R. "A Pattern of Development in Moral Judgments Made by Adolescents Derived from Piaget's Schema of its Development in Childhood." *Educational Review* 19 (1966): 79-98.
Macrae, D. "A Test of Piaget's Theories of Moral Development." *Journal of Abnormal and Social Psychology* 49 (1954): 14-18.
Mischel, Theodore. "Piaget: Cognitive Conflict and the Motivation of Thought." In *Cognitive Development and Epistemology.* Edited by T. Mischel. New York: Academic Press, 1971.
Piaget, Jean. *The Moral Judgment of the Child.* London: Routledge and Kegan Paul, 1932.
————. *The Child's Conception of the World.* New York: Harcourt, Brace, 1929.


D. Kohlberg's theory and related studies:

Frishkin, J.; Keniston, K.; and MacKinnon, C. "Moral Reasoning and Political Ideology." *Journal of Personality and Social Psychology* 27 (1973): 109-119.
Haan, N.; Smith M. B.; and Block, J. "The Moral Reasoning of Young Adults." *Journal of Personality and Social Psychology* 10 (1968): 183-201.
Kohlberg, Lawrence. "From Is to Ought." In *Cognitive Development and Epistemology.* Edited by T. Mischel. New York: Academic Press, 1971, pp. 131-256.
————. "Stages of Moral Development as a Basis for Moral Education. In *Moral Education.* Edited by C. M. Beck, B. S. Crittenden, and E. V. Sullivan. Toronto: University of Toronto Press, 1971, pp. 23-92.
————. "Stage and Sequence: The Cognitive Development Approach to Socialization." In *Handbook of Socialization Theory and Research.* Edited by D. A. Goslin. Chicago: Rand McNally, 1969, pp. 347-480.
Kohlberg, L., and Gilligan, C. "The Adolescent as a Philosopher: The Discovery of

the Self in a Postconventional World." *Daedalus* 100 (Fall 1971): 1051-86.

Kohlberg, L., and Mayer, R. "Development as the Aim of Education." *Harvard Education Review* 42 (1972): 449-96.

Rest, James; Turiel, E.; and Kohlberg, L. "Levels of Moral Development as a Determinant of Preference and Comprehension of Moral Judgments Made by Others." *Journal of Personality* 37 (1969): 225-52.

Turiel, E. "Developmental Processes in the Child's Moral Thinking." In *Trends and Issues in Developmental Psychology*. Edited by P. Mussen, J. Langer, and M. Covington. New York: Holt, Rinehart and Winston, 1969, pp. 93-131.

————. Turiel, E. "An Experimental Test of the Sequentiality of Developmental Stages in the Child's Moral Judgments." *Journal of Personality and Social Psychology* 3 (1966): 611-18.


E. For critical comments on the Kohlberg theory see the works listed below in section F by Williams and Williams, Wright, and Kay, and the following articles:


Alston, William P. "Comments on Kohlberg's 'From Is to Ought.'" In *Cognitive Development and Epistemology*. Edited by T. Mischel. New York: Academic Press, 1971, pp. 269-85.

Aronfreed, J. "Some Problems for a Theory of the Acquisition of Conscience." In *Moral Education*. Edited by C. M. Beck, B. S. Crittenden, and E. V. Sullivan. Toronto: University of Toronto Press, 1971, pp. 183-99.

Bergman, M. "Moral Decision Making in the Light of Kohlberg and Bonhoeffer." *Religious Education* 69 (1974): 227-42.

Crittenden, B. S., ed. "Discussion." In *Moral Education*. Edited by C. M. Beck, B. S. Crittenden, and E. V. Sullivan. Toronto: University of Toronto Press, 1971.

Peters, Richard S. "Moral Developments: A Plea for Pluralism." In *Cognitive Development and Epistemology*. Edited by T. Mischel. New York: Academic Press, 1971, pp. 237-68.

Simpson, Elizabeth L. "Moral Development Research: A Case Study of Scientific Cultural Bias." *Human Development* 17 (1974): 81-106.


F. Accounts of other cognitive-development theories are found in:


Baldwin, A. L. "A Cognitive Theory of Socialization." In *Handbook of Socialization Theory and Research*. Edited by D. A. Goslin. Chicago: Rand McNally, 1968, pp. 325-46.

Brennen, W. K. "The Foundations for Moral Development." *Special Education* 54 (1965).

Bull, Norman J. *Moral Judgment from Childhood to Adolescence*. London: Routledge and Kegan Paul, 1969.

Edwards, J. B. "Some Studies of the Moral Development of Children." *Educational Research* 7 (1965): 200-211.

Kay, W. *Moral Development.* London: Allen and Unwin, 1968.

Morris, J. F. "The Development of Adolescent Value-Judgments." *British Journal of Educational Psychology* 28 (1958): 1-14.

Williams, Norman, and Williams, Sheila. *The Moral Development of Children.* London: Macmillan, 1970.

Wright, Derek. *The Psychology of Moral Behaviour.* Baltimore, Md.: Penguin, 1971.

G. Other works on moral development:

Bryan, J. H., and London, P. "Altruistic Behaviour by Children." *Psychological Bulletin* 73 (1970): 200-211.

Cowan, P. A.; Langer, J.; Heavenrich, J.; and Nathanson, M. "Social Learning and Piaget's Theory of Moral Development." *Journal of Personality and Social Psychology* 11 (1969): 261-74.

Durkheim, Émile. *Moral Education.* New York: Free Press, 1960.

Durkin, D. "The Specificity of Children's Moral Judgments." *Journal of Genetic Psychology* 98 (1961): 3-13.

Hartshorne, H.; May, M. A.; and Maller, J. B. *Studies in the Nature of Character.* 3 vols. New York: Macmillan, 1928-32.

Havighurst, R. J., and Taba, H. *Adolescent Character and Personality.* New York: Wiley, 1949.

Lerner, E. *Constraint Areas and the Moral Judgment of Children.* Menasha, Wisconsin: George Banta, 1937.

Medinnus, G. R. "Behavioral and Cognitive Measures of Conscience Development." *Journal of Genetic Psychology* 109 (1966): 147-50.

Peck, R. F., and Havighurst, R. J. *The Psychology of Character Development.* New York: Wiley, 1960.

## V. HUMANISTIC PSYCHOLOGY AND EDUCATION

Allen, P. M., et al. *Teacher Self-Appraisal: A Way of Looking Over Your Own Shoulder.* Worthington, Ohio: Charles A. Jones, 1970.

Argyle, Michael. *The Psychology of Interpersonal Behaviour.* Baltimore, Md.: Penguin, 1967.

Brown, G. I. *Human Teaching for Human Learning.* New York: Viking, 1971.

Crary, R. *Humanizing the School.* New York: Knopf, 1969.

Engle, S. H., and Longstreet, W. S. *A Design for Social Education in the Open Curriculum.* New York: Harper and Row, 1972.

Gordon, T. *Parent Effectiveness Training.* New York: Peter H. Wyden, 1970.

Harris, T. A. *I'm O.K.—You're O.K.: A Practical Guide to Transactional Analysis.* New York: Harper and Row, 1967.

Hunter, E. *Encounter in the Classroom: New Ways of Teaching.* New York: Holt, Rinehart and Winston, 1972.

Karlin, M. S., and Berger, R. *Experiential Learning.* West Nyack, N.Y.: Parker, 1971.

Kohl, Herbert. *The Open Classroom.* New York: The New York Review, 1969.

Krathwohl, D. R.; Bloom, B.S.; and Masia, B. B. *Taxonomy of Educational Objectives: Handbook II: Affective Domain.* New York: David McKay, 1964.

Macy, C. *Let's Teach Them Right.* Buffalo, N.Y.: Prometheus, 1973.

Maslow, Abraham H. *Toward a Psychology of Being.* New York: Van Nostrand Reinhold, 1968.

Nyquist, E. B., and Hawes, G. R., eds. *Open Education.* New York: Bantam, 1972.

Patterson, C. H. *Humanistic Education.* Englewood Cliffs, N.J.: Prentice-Hall, 1973.

Rich, J. M. *Education and Human Values.* Reading, Mass.: Addison Wesley Publishing Co., 1968.

Rogers, Carl R. *Freedom to Learn.* Columbus, Ohio: Charles E. Merrill, 1969.

————. *Client-Centered Therapy: Its Current Practice, Implications, and Theory.* Boston: Houghton Mifflin, 1951.

————. "A Theory of Therapy, Personality, and Interpersonal Relations, as Developed in the Client-Centered Framework." In *Psychology: A Study of a Science.* Vol. 3. Edited by S. Koch. New York: McGraw-Hill, 1959.

Stanford, G., and Roark, A. E. *Human Interaction in Education.* Boston: Allyn and Bacon, 1974.

Zahorik, J. A., and Brubaker, D. L. *Toward More Humanistic Instruction.* Dubuque, Iowa: Wm. C. Brown, 1972.

## VI. TEACHING AND LEARNING RESOURCES

A. Case study methods and materials:

Clark, H. "A Report on the Use of the Case Study Method by Members of the American Society for Christian Ethics." Mimeographed, American Society for Christian Ethics, 1969.

Galbraith, Ronald E., and Jones, Tom M. *Teaching Strategies for Moral Dilemmas.* Pittsburgh, Pa.: Social Studies Curriculum Center, Carnegie-Mellon University, 1974.

Garrett, T. M., et al. *Cases in Business Ethics.* New York: Holt, Rinehart and Winston, 1968.

McNair, M. P., ed. *The Case Method at the Harvard Business School.* New York: McGraw-Hill, 1954.

B. Discussion skills and techniques:

Barnlund, D. C., and Haiman, F. S. *The Dynamics of Discussion*. Boston: Houghton Mifflin, 1960.

Cortright, R. L., and Hinds, G. L. *Creative Discussion*. New York: Macmillan, 1959.

Hoover, K. H. *Learning and Teaching in the Secondary School*. Boston: Allyn and Bacon, 1968.

Keltner, J. W. *Group Discussion Processes*. London: Longmans, Green, 1957.

Raths, Louis; Harmin, M.; and Simon, S. *Values and Teaching*. Columbus, Ohio: Charles E. Merrill, 1966.

Robinson, D. "Scraps from a Teacher's Notebook." *Phi Delta Kappan* 48 (October 1966).

Sanders, N. M. *Classroom Questions: What Kinds?* New York: Harper and Row, 1966.

Stanford, B., and Stanford, G. *Learning Discussion Skills Through Games*. New York: Citation Press, 1969.

Wagner, R. H., and Arnold, C. C. *Handbook of Group Discussion*. Boston: Houghton Mifflin, 1950.

C. Role play resources:

Adult Education Association of the U.S.A. "How to Use Role Playing and Other Tools for Learning." Leadership Pamphlet No. 6. Chicago, 1955.

Flavell, J. H. *The Development of Role-taking and Communication Skills in Children*. New York: Wiley, 1968.

Haas, R. B., ed. *Psychodrama and Sociodrama in American Education*. New York: Beacon House, 1949.

Hawley, R. C. *Value Exploration Through Role Play*. Amherst, Mass.: E R A Press, 1974.

Klein, A. F. *How to Use Role-Playing Effectively*. New York: Association Press, 1974.

Schmuck, R. A., and Schmuck, P. A. *Group Processes in the Classroom*. Dubuque, Iowa: Wm. C. Brown, 1971.

Shaftel, F. R., and Shaftel, G. *Role-Playing for Social Values: Decision-Making in the Social Studies*. Englewood Cliffs, N.J.: Prentice-Hall, 1967.

D. Resources on games and simulations:

Abt, C. C. *Serious Games*. New York: Viking Press, 1970.

*Games and Simulations*. London: British Broadcasting Corporation, 1973. Especially helpful is the catalog of games available. It also includes an extensive bibliography.

Greenblatt, C. S.; Stein, P. J.; and Washburne, N. F. *The Marriage Game: Understanding Marital Decision-Making*. New York; Random House, 1974.

Mobley and Associates. *Valuing Simulation*. Mobley and Associates, 5000 Sheppard Lane, Ellicott City, Md., 21043.